QuickTest Professional (QTP)

Version 10

Interview Questions and Guidelines

Reference Guide

by

Sridhar R Mallepally
MCA, MA, M.Ed.

QuickTest Professional (QTP) Interview Questions and Guidelines

90 Tufts Dr., Manchester, CT 06042

International Standard Book Number: 978-0979147906

Printed in the United States of America

First Printing: July 2009

Disclaimer

This material, questions and answers to these questions are prepared out of experience of the author and author takes no responsibility for authenticity or accuracy of the material provided.

This is not a tutorial and author expects the readers to have minimum knowledge of software industry and know how to use the testing tool QuickTest professional. QuickTest professional, WinRunner, Quality Center and TestDirector are the products and trademarks of Mercury Interactive/HP Software. Snapshots in this document are the courtesy of HP Software.

Acknowledgements

This book is the result of my collective experience in the field of test automation with the Mercury Interactive/HP Software at various clients across the United States and I thank everyone for giving me the opportunity to gain this experience.

I also take this opportunity to thank all my students who encouraged me to write this book with their successful entry into the testing field.

I give credit to Mercury Interactive/HP Software for the snapshots of various QTP tool images for illustrations and for the snapshots of their sample training applications used in this book.

Last but not the least I am thankful to my loving wife Samatha and lovely Son Rishi, for being so co-operative with me while I was preparing this book.

Table of Contents

Overview and Scope

a. Purpose

This book is intended to provide the guidelines and best practices to follow in building reusable and robust QTP scripts for every aspect of the application testing.

b. Target Audience

This book is intended for use by the automation engineers. Prior knowledge of QTP will be very helpful in understanding this document. Author advises the users to go through the tutorial provided with QTP before following the examples given in this book.

c. Constraints

The automation guidelines described here are to reap the long term benefits and are not intended for one time testing efforts.

This document is prepared keeping in view the industry standards and may be modified from time to time based on the behavior and flow of the application.

Business Component Settings are not covered in this document as it is out of scope.

Frequently Asked Questions with answers

1.1.Introduction to QuickTest Professional:

What is QuickTest Professional?

QuickTest Professional is a Functional and Regression testing tool from HP Software, which can record the user actions, keyed in while recording and execute these user actions while we play back (run) the test. It can be used to test the functionality of the application in the regression testing phase.

How do you decide what test cases to be automated?

When we have a large number of test cases (in most cases we do) we have to carefully analyze them and group them into categories and then decide if that test case should executed on every release/build of the application or not. If the test case is not intended to be executed on every release it should not be automated since it falls into a "one-time" testing category.
Some test cases might be very time consuming to automate where as executing them manually could be just a matter of 5 to 10 minutes. Such type of test cases should be given the least priority in terms of when to automate them. Some test cases may have manual intervention for example: when you create an account in the application someone in your team has to do run some batch processes manually in order for you to continue with further testing. These kind of test cases should not be automated unless you have full control of the backend processes to be run for successful completion of the test using QTP.

How does QTP work?

QTP has two components:

a) VB Script Language

b) Object Repository

While recording the user actions on the applications QTP will generate the VB Script statements, which indicate the actions it is supposed to perform.
While recording, QTP will also learn the objects present in the application, say for example a Window, check box, radio button etc., and stores these objects in a place called Object Repository. In order to run the test successfully the corresponding object should exist in the Object Repository.

1.2. Recording QTP Scripts:

What are the modes of Recording in QTP?

There are three modes:

- Context Sensitive,
- Low Level
- Analog.

Context Sensitive Mode:

In this mode QTP records the objects and properties of the objects from the application so that it can identify them while playing back the script. 99% of testing is done using the context sensitive mode.

Analog mode:

In this mode QTP records the mouse movements and key strokes on the keyboard as Tracks so that it can help you in testing the situations like signature scanning or handwriting or drawing some objects on the screen or in a window etc.

Low Level recording:

In this mode QTP records the objects based on their location by capturing the X and Y coordinates of the objects on the screen.
The Analog and Low Level recording modes can be selected only after hitting the record button. In the picture below the First icon is for Analog recording and the second one is for Low Level recording.

Analog and Low Level Recording modes can only be selected after starting to Record and going to the Automation menu.

1.3. Playback of QTP Scripts:

What are the modes of running test in QTP and what do they mean?

There are three modes of replaying the test. These are not listed on the tool bar.

When we hit the Run button we get the "Run" dialogue box, which gives us two options.

1. To save the results in New run results folder. This is the Verify mode.
2. To save the results in Temporary run results folder overwriting the earlier results. This is the Debug mode.
3. When we need to run the test to update the Checkpoints go to "Automation" menu and select "Update Run Mode".

1). Verify Mode:

If the test engineer wants to save the results of the test run to compare and verify with the future runs of the same test he would go with the Verify mode.

2). Debug Mode:

If the Test engineer does not want to save the results as he is yet to finish the script or he is testing his QTP coding logic he would run the test in the debug mode.

3). Update Mode:

If a test engineer wants to update the expected results while running the test, say for example while recording the script the calendar date was 10/20/2008 and while executing the test it is a different date (system date), then the test should be run in the update mode otherwise the test would fail because of the changed properties of the object.

Sequence of things happening when the script is played back:

1. QTP's inbuilt interpreter checks for the syntax errors in the script.
2. It checks to see if the object specified in the script exists in the repository.
3. It checks if the object specified in the script exists on the Application Under Test.
4. Does the action/task specified in the script.

   During script execution if any of the above phases encounter the error, then an error window pops up depending on the situation.

   Snapshots of the error messages:

1. Syntax error:

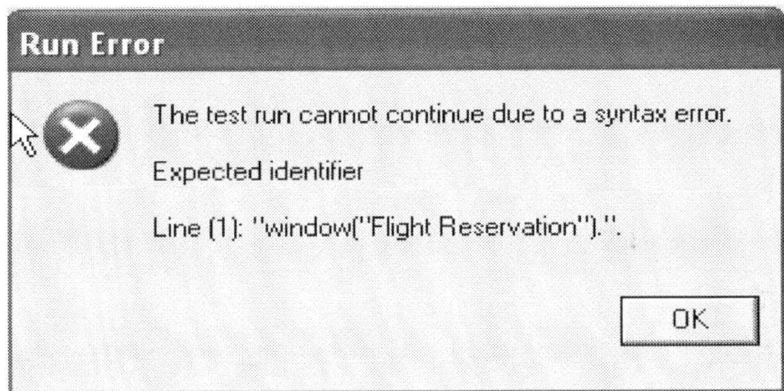

2. Object not found in the repository:

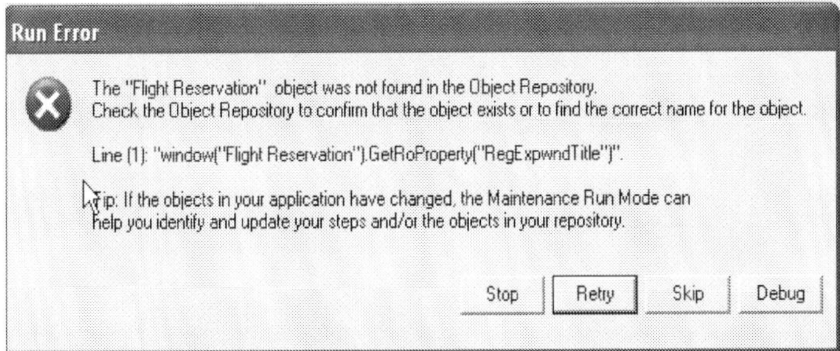

3. **Object exists in the repository but is not displayed on the screen:**

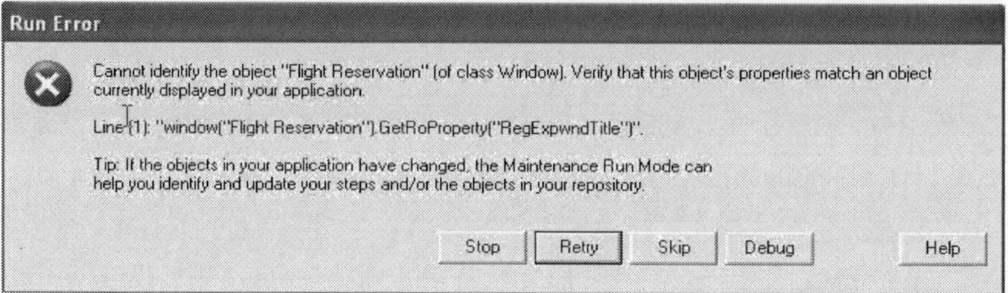

1.4. Working with Application Under Test:

How do you start the Application Under Test?

If you are working with just one application:

In QTP we can specify the URL for the application or the exe file of the application within the settings. Go to "Automation" menu and select "Record and Run Settings" option. It opens a Record and Run settings dialogue box, which has options to enter the URL of the application for web or exe file of the application if it is windows application.

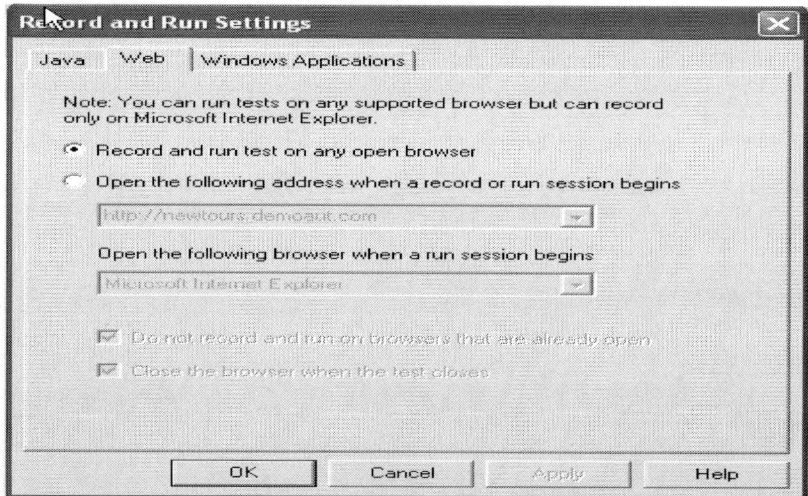

For the main test, which calls the reusable actions, we can use the option "Open the following browser when a record or run session begins". Once the application is open we don't need to open the application again so for all the reusable action we can use the option "Record and run test on any open

Web browser". But we should make sure that all the browsers except Quality Center are closed before recording or running the tests.

For windows applications we can select the application by clicking the "Add" button and browsing the 0065xecutable file of the application.
See the picture below:

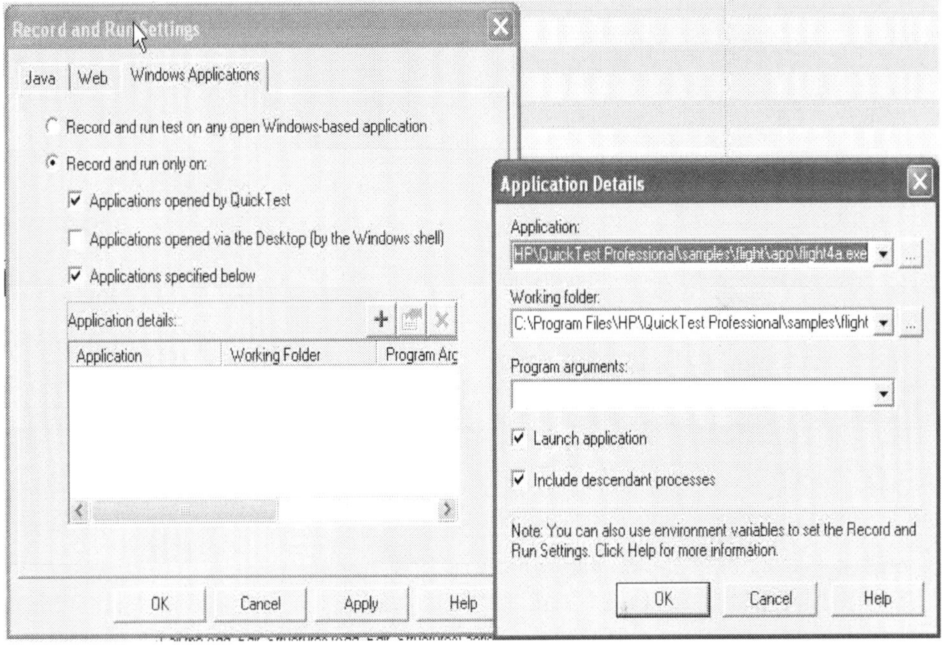

If you are working with multiple applications:

At workplace usually we will be working with more than one application and we might need to automate the test cases for these applications. In this situation we should select the Radio button "Record and run test on any windows based application" for non web based application or "record and run test on any open browsers" for web applications which will instruct QTP not to open any application by itself. Then we need to include the statement SystemUtil.Run in the Login script /Action and execute that as the first action in the flow of actions.

Example: SystemUtil.Run http://www.onsitetraining.net

Or if it is a windows based application we have to give the path of the executable.

```
SystemUtil.Run "C:\Program Files\Mercury Interactive\QuickTest Professional\samples\flight\app\flight4a.exe"
```

What statement would you use to send the results to the test results?

We would use Reporter.Reportevent followed by the step name, description and result to send the result to the test results and get the status whether the step passed or failed.

Example:

Reporter.ReportEvent 0,"Property Check", "Property Checked Passed"

Value "0" indicates that the step is passed and "1" indicates that the step is failed. You can also use micPass or micFail in place of 0 or 1.

1.5. Parameterization:

What is Parameterization?

Parameterization is a way of data entry into the application without hard coding the values within the test script.

There are various ways to parameterize.

i) Using values from Data Table

ii) Using Environment Variables

iii) Using Random Numbers generated

iv) Using Test Parameters

v) Using Action Parameters

What are the standard Object classes?

Developers assign properties to each object on the application. Object class is an industry standard to identify a particular type of object in the application and some of the commonly used standard classes are:

- Window
- Dialog box

- Menu
- Push button
- Edit Box
- Checkbox
- Radio button
- List box
- Combo box

If the class property of the object is defined as Object or WinObject or WebElement depending on the type of application you are using, then it is not a standard object and comes under the category of Non-Standard object.

How do you identify an object if it is not associated with any standard class, using QTP?

Any object which is not associated with the standard class will have a class of either WinObject (for Windows applications) or WebElement (for web applications) and are considered as Non-Standard objects. Non-standard objects are represented with a special Tri-colored symbol in the Object Repository.

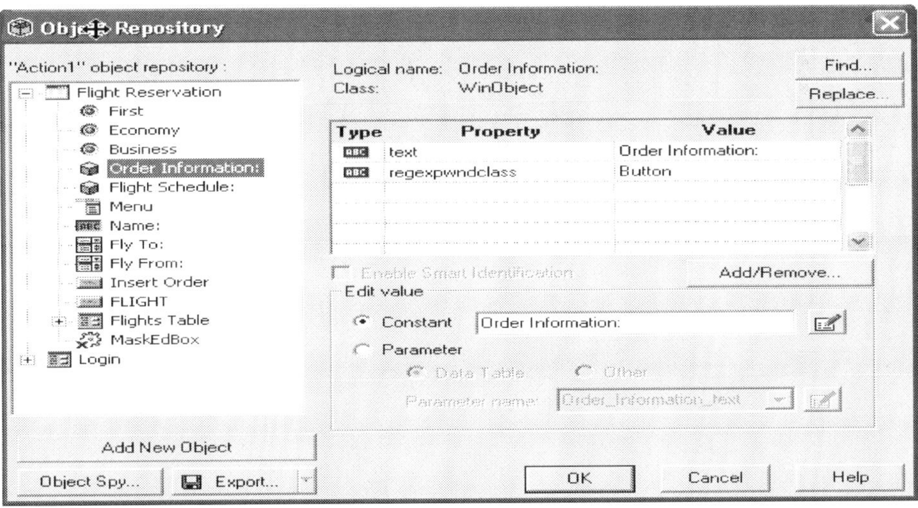

1.6. Object Repository:

What is an Object Repository?

Object Repository (OR) is a collection of objects pertaining to the application under test. Example: All the text boxes, list boxes, images etc are stored in a file in QTP. This file is called the object repository. Each object will have the set of properties to identify that object uniquely in the application. At the time of execution, QTP identifies the objects on the screen by comparing them with the objects and their properties in the repository.

What are the types of Object Repositories in QTP and how do we define them?

QTP has two types of Object Repositories.

1. Action Local repository
2. Shared Object Repository

We can have any number of Shared Object Repositories associated with an action. All the objects will be recorded into the local repository and we need to export the objects from local repository into the shared object repository by opening the object repository and selecting File Menu and selecting "Export Local Objects". You need to specify the name for the shared object repository in which you want to save these objects.

Associating multiple Object repositories for a test:

Open the object repository of the action and click on the icon Associate Repositories  on the tool bar. Associate repositories window opens. Click on the green "+" sign and browse the shared object repository and select it. All the actions which are available in that script will be shown in the Available Actions section of that window. Select the action which you to associate the repositories to and click on the ">" arrow to send it to the "Associated Actions" section of the window. This will ensure that the actions in the associated actions will have access to all the objects in the associated object repositories. You can associate any number of object repositories.

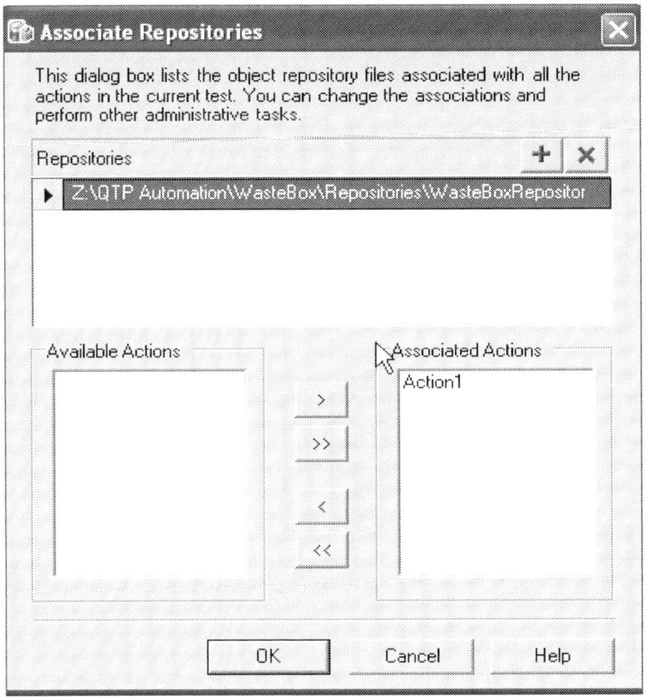

Differentiate between the two modes: Object Repository Per Action Mode and Shared Object Repository Mode.

Local Object Repository Mode

In this mode there is no need to save the Object repository. It is automatically loaded with the script and saved into the script folder. The effort to maintain Object Repository is relatively less, but if we have a lot of tests we get confused with the Object Repositories and when a change is made in application it has to be modified in all the Object Repositories.

Shared Object Repository Mode

We can have the luxury of having just one Shared Object Repository no matter how many tests we have. We can associate the same repository for every action or test. Whenever an object's property is changed we can just change that in one Object Repository and all the tests will be fine.

What are Object Properties?

Most Objects will have two types of properties defined within the application.

a. Identification Properties
b. Native Properties

The properties defined for the object in the application can be discovered by using the object spy icon which is on the toolbar or from "Tools" menu select Object Spy.

Identification Properties:

These are the properties which an object attains based on the condition within the application. Example: The FLIGHT button is designed to have a runtime/Identification property of enabled=False when we open the Flight reservation window and once we select the Date and fly from and fly to this objects runtime property is designed to change the enabled=True. These are dynamic values which can keep changing.

Native Properties:

These are the properties defined within the application for each object which will act as base properties and they may not change dynamically.

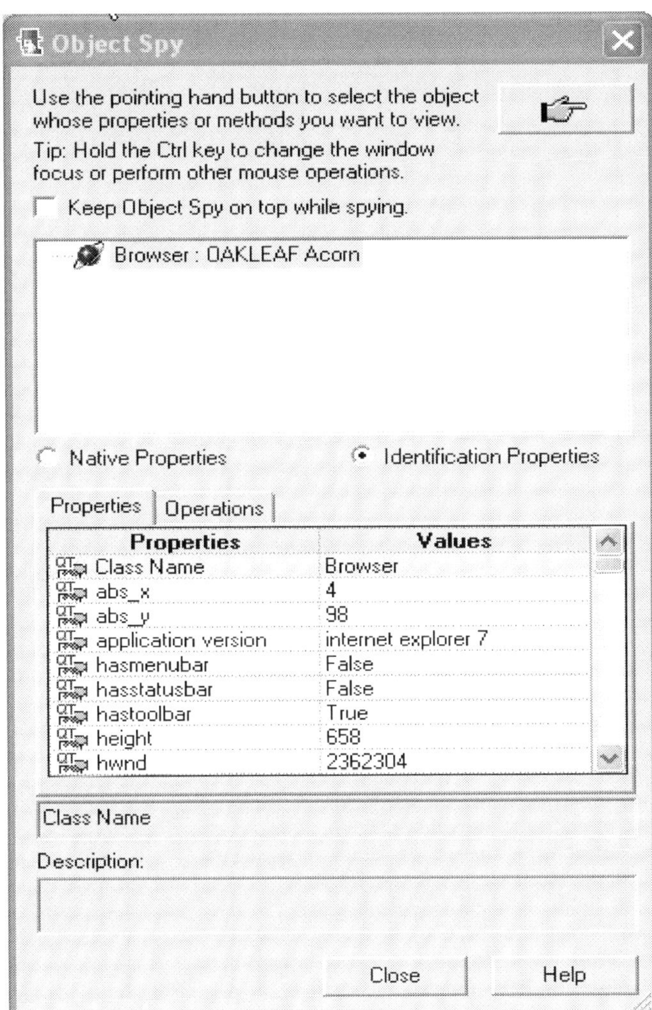

1.7. Functions in QuickTest Professional:

What is a Function ?

Function is a program which takes in the arguments or parameters and does the steps specified in the program and ultimately gives you an output.

```
ActualStatus =  window("Flight Reservation").WinButton(ButtonName).GetROProperty("enabled")
If ActualStatus= ExpectedStatus Then
    Reporter.ReportEvent micPass,"Verify Flight Button","Flight button was disabled as expected"
else
    Reporter.ReportEvent micFail,"Verify Flight Button","Flight button was enabled but the expected was disabled"
End If
End Function
```

Function Call: VerifyButtonStatus "FLIGHT",False

Return Value:

A function should return a value in most cases. This return value can be used in the script where the function is being called for various reasons. A return value should be returning either a variable from the function or value calculated in the function or any value string which you specify within the function such as “Pass” or “Fail”. To return a return value give the function name = Value to be returned.

Example:

If the return value given by Login function is “Pass” or “True” you may want to continue further testing else you may want to end the test if it returns a value of “Fail” or “False”.

```
var_FlightLogin = FlightLogin("sridhar", "mercury")
If  var_FlightLogin = "Pass" Then
  RunAction "OrderEntry [OrderEntry]", allIterations
  RunAction "FlightLogout [FlightLogout]", oneIteration
else
  ExitActionIteration()
End If
```

Can we have a separate function library for QTP?

Yes, QTP functions can be written and stored in a VB Script file which has an extension of .vbs (plain text file stored with an extension of .vbs) and we can

attach that file in the "File" →"Settings" →"Resources" and under resources we have the top most section which says "Associated library files". Click on the "+" sign in that section and browse the VB Script file which has the functions you created.
Example: 'Function to close all browsers before starting the test execution can be given as:
call CloseAllBrowsers()
or simply CloseAllBrowsers()

All the functions should be stored in a common function library. Open a blank notepad file. Paste all your functions in that and save that file with an extension .vbs and with a name which can identify it as a function library (Example: FlightFunctionLibrary). Save this file under a new folder called "FunctionLibraries" in the project folder.
VBS stands for Visual Basic Script.
Once you save the library go to QTP and select Settings from the File menu. Test Settings window appears. Go to Resources Tab. You will see a section called Function Libraries. Click on the Green "+" sign in that and browse your function library which you saved in the project folder. Now all the functions present in that library will be available to all the scripts with this settings. You can save any number of functions in one .vbs file but for maintenance purposes it is better to limit the number to 50 functions or build a separate function library for each module within the application if these modules are large modules.
Where ever we need to call a function press F7 and the Step generator window will open. From the top drop down, select Functions and then from the second drop down, select library functions. Now you will be able to see a list of all the functions present in all the libraries which you attached to that script. Select the function which you need to use, give the arguments and press Insert button. The function call will be inserted in your script at the cursor position.

Here are a few sample functions: **(You can use any VB scripting functions in QTP. Go through the VB Scripting documents available to you)**

```
'##############################################################
'This function returns the maximum number of days in a month.
'##############################################################
Function NoOfDaysInMonth(InMonth)
Dim NoOfDays
   Select Case InMonth
      Case "01", "1", "03", "3", "05", "5", "07", "7", "08", "8", "10", "12"
                  NoOfDaysInMonth = "31"
      Case "02", "2"
                  NoOfDaysInMonth = "28"
      Case "04", "4", "06", "6", "09", "9", "11"
                  NoOfDaysInMonth = "30"
      Case Else
         NoOfDaysInMonth =  "The value passed is an illegal parameter"
   End Select
End Function

'##############################################################
'This function changes the date according to the parameters
'##############################################################
Function ChangeDate(dttochange,mm, dd, yyyy)
      Dim DateArray, NewDate
      If mm = "" Then
                  mm = 0
      End If
      If dd = "" Then
                  dd = 0
      End If
      If yyyy = "" Then
                  yyyy = 0
      End If
      NewDate = DateAdd("m",mm,dttochange)
      NewDate = DateAdd("d",dd,NewDate)
      NewDate = DateAdd("yyyy",yyyy,NewDate)
      DateArray = Split(NewDate, "/")
      Mth = DateArray(0)
      Dt = DateArray(1)
      Yr = DateArray(2)
      If Mth<10 Then
        Mth = "0"&Mth
      End If
```

```
        If Dt<10 Then
                Dt = "0"&Dt
        End If
        NewDate = Mth&"/"&Dt&"/"&Yr
        ChangeDate = NewDate
End Function
```

'##

'This function closes all open browsers except Test Director & Quality Center

'##

```
Function CloseAllBrowsers()
Dim vcol_Handles, vCtr, vHwnd, Flag, vLastHWnd
vCtr = 0
Flag = 1
Set vcol_Handles = CreateObject("Scripting.Dictionary")
While (Window("regexpwndclass:=IEFrame","index:=" & vCtr).Exist And Flag)
        wait 1
        vHwnd = Window("regexpwndclass:=IEFrame","index:=" & vCtr).getroproperty("Hwnd")
        If (vLastHWnd=vHwnd) Then
                Flag = 0
        Else
                vcol_Handles.Add CStr(vcol_Handles.Count),vHwnd
                vCtr = vCtr+1
        End If
                vLastHWnd = vHwnd
        Wend

'Use reverse order in this for loop so that the text and Hwnd remain in correct order after each is closed
For vCtr = vcol_Handles.Count-1 to 0 step -1
Wait 1
vHwnd = vcol_Handles.Item(CStr(vCtr))
vBrowser = Window("regexpwndclass:=IEFrame","index:=" & vCtr).getroproperty("text")
If Instr(vBrowser, "TestDirector") or Instr(vBrowser, "Quality Center") then
        Reporter.ReportEvent 2, "Not closed " & vBrowser, "The browser '" & vBrowser & "' was not closed"
Else
        Reporter.ReportEvent 2, "Closed " & vBrowser, "The browser '" &        vBrowser & "' was closed"
        Window("hwnd:=" & vHwnd).Close
End If
        Next
End Function
```

```
'For the below function to work you have to manually add the web element to your OR.
'###################################################################
'This function checks the screen name
###################################################################
Function ScreenCheck(ScreenName)
Rc= Browser("Browser").Page("Page").WebElement(ScreenName).GetROProperty("innertext")
If Rc = ScreenName Then
      Reporter.ReportEvent micpass, "screen check", ScreenName&" screen appeared"
      ScreenCheck = "Pass"
 Else
      Reporter.ReportEvent micfail, "screen check", ScreenName&" screen did not appear"
      ScreenCheck = "Fail"
      ExitGlobalIteration() 'Goes to next row in the Global Table (or next      test case).
 End If
End Function

Example:  ScreenCheck("Restrictions") ' Where "Restrictions" is the name of the screen.
```

How can you map a custom class to a standard class in QTP?

Custom object is an object which is not recognized by QTP and it is recorded as WinObject, but if you think it can be used as a standard object such as edit field or radio button we can map it to that standard class.
Select Tools → Object Identification. In the Object Identification dialogue box select Standard windows in the Environment box. The user-defined box will now be enabled. Click User Defined. The object mapping dialogue box opens. Click the hand icon and click on the object whose class you want to add to user-defined class. In the Map to box select the standard object class to which you want to map this user-defined object.

How would you split a date, which is in the format "mm/dd/yyyy"?

DateArray = Split(**Date**, "/")

MyDate = Datearray(0)&"-"& Datearray(1)&"-"&Datearray(2)

MsgBox MyDate

Date gives the today's date.

In this "/" is the delimiter. DateArray will store the values which can be used as displayed by MsgBox and concatenated together as a single variable MyDate as shown above.

Note:

MsgBox is for displaying the variable value. You should delete or comment all the lines with MsgBox once you are done fixing your script.

How can you see if you are getting the right value into the variables?

We can use MsgBox followed by variable and the test will pause and show the value present in the variable. The other way is, using the debug viewer where you can see the value of each variable in the runtime. To activate debug viewer select Debug viewer from view menu or click on the icon for Debug Viewer represented by the spectacles (eye glasses) on the toolbar.

1.8. Data Driven Testing:

What is Data Driven Testing?

Data Driven Testing is a process of entering variable values into the application taking them from the data sheet.

Variable values can be passed into QTP through the Global sheet or local sheet depending on the architecture you are using. The easy way to parameterize the data is through the Keyword view.

From the keyword view select the object whose value you want to pass through the data table. Click in the Value column for that row and you will see a little <#> sign in the right hand corner of that cell. Click on that and Value Configuration Options window will open. This will have two main radio buttons Constant and Parameter. You can see the current value present in the Constant edit field. Select the Parameter radio button. Select DataTable from the drop down next to parameter. (You can also select the other two options present in the drop down Environment or Random Number.). Now enter the field name from which you want to select the data. If that field doesn't exist QTP will create one for you. Then select from which data table you want to enter the data. You can enter the data either from the Global sheet or Current action sheet (local table). Now click "OK". The field will be created for you and the data for that field is taken from the data table instead of having a hard coded value within the script.

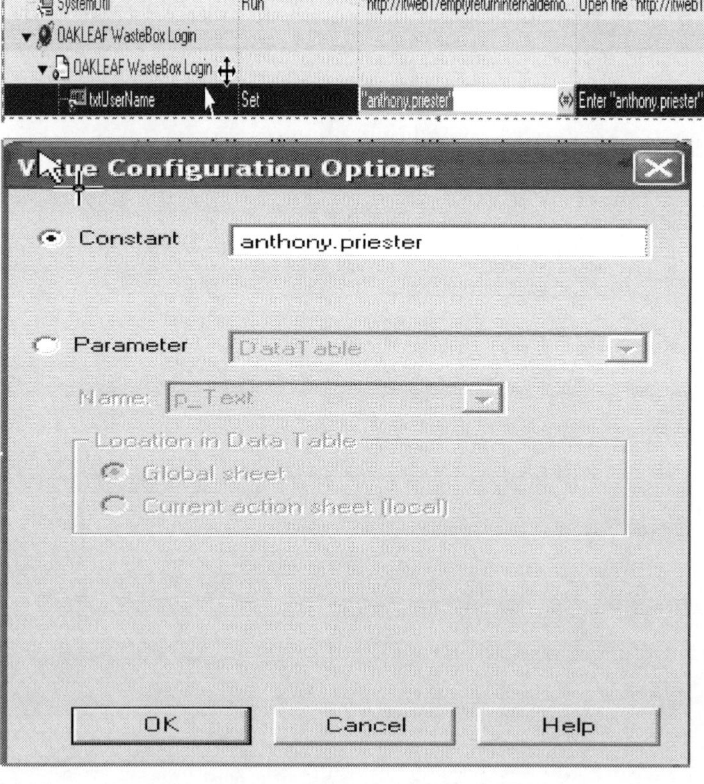

What are the statements you would use to get the values from the application into your variables?

We can use GetROProperty and specify what property of the object you want to get into the variable.

Example:

In this example after recording the Radio button “trip type” we want to send the message to the test results.

In example 1 we are sending the result of property check. If the “selected item index” property of the radio button is “1” which is “round trip” we are passing the test else we are failing the test.

Example 1:

```
xxx= Browser("Find a Flight:").Page("Find a Flight:").WebRadioGroup("tripType").GetROProperty("selected item index")
MsgBox xxx
If xxx = 1 Then
      Reporter.ReportEvent 0,"Property Check", "Property Checked Passed"
else
      Reporter.ReportEvent 1,"Property Check", "Property Checked Failed"
End If
```

In example 2 we are sending the result of which item is checked based on the property “selected item index”. If the “selected item index” property of the radio button is “1” which is “round trip” we are sending that message to results and if it “2” we are sending that “One way” is selected to the test results.

Example 2:

```
xxx= Browser("Find a Flight:").Page("Find a Flight:").WebRadioGroup("tripType").GetROProperty("selected item index")
MsgBox xxx
If xxx = 1 Then
      Reporter.ReportEvent 0,"Selected Item Check", "Round Trip is selected"
else
      If xxx = 2 Then
```

```
        Reporter.ReportEvent 0," Selected Item Check", "Oneway trip is
selected"
    End If
End If
```

Can we write the data into data table, using QTP?

Yes. We can write the data grabbed into the variables. This is done during the record mode. Start the record session and from the "Insert" menu select "Output Value" and based on the type of object we need to select either Standard Output value or Text output value. For example if the object is a list item or edit box select Standard output value. QTP will then show the object properties and now we need to select what property we want to output. In this case it is the "Value". Also we need to specify the field name into which we want to send the value and the data table whether Global sheet or local sheet. QTP will suggest you a field name you can either accept or change it according to your naming convention.

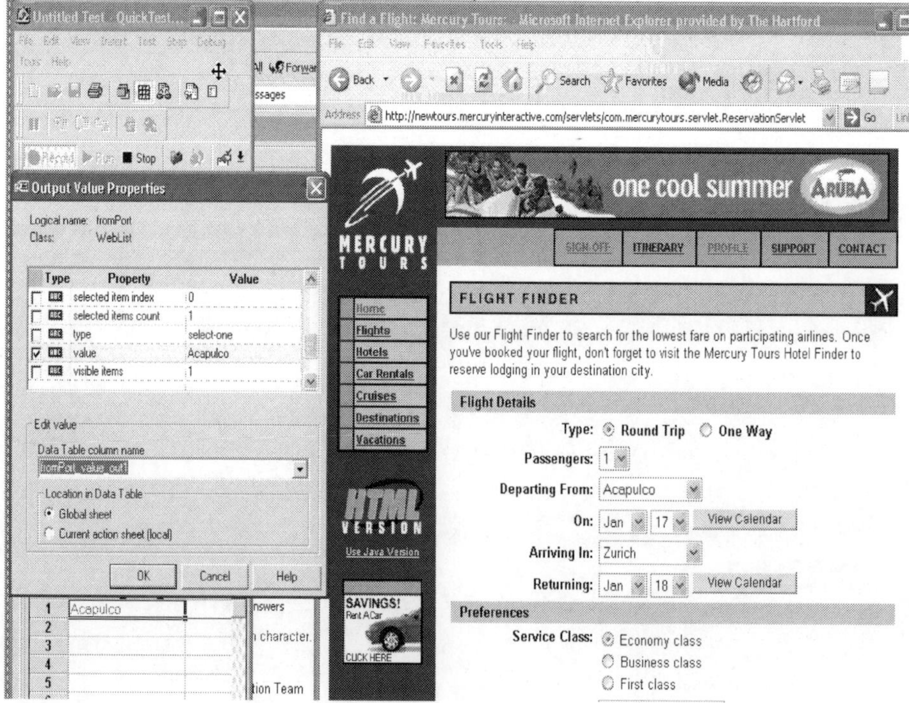

If the Text we want to capture is the text displayed on the screen by the application use the "Text Output Value" and point the text, which you want to capture and give the appropriate field name and table.

Note: This output value is shown only in the runtime and once the test execution is finished the data can't be seen in the data table. But you can see the data in the Runtime data table in the results.

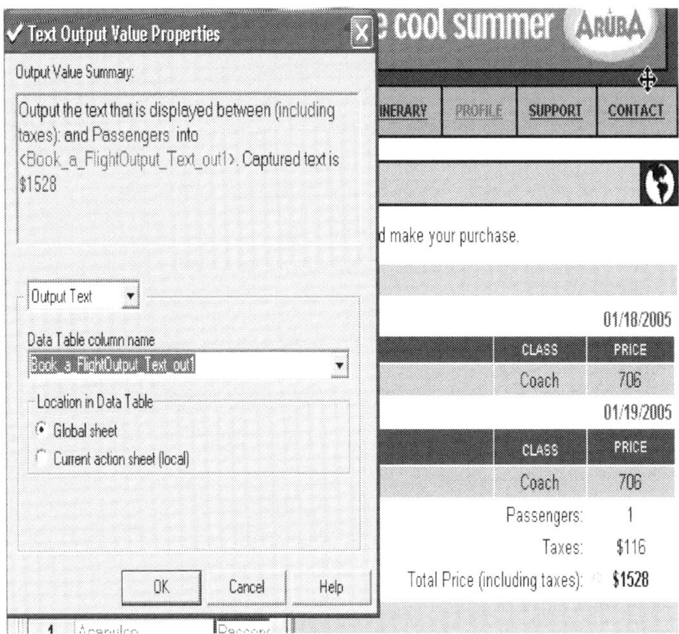

Sending the variable values to the data table.

The variable values can be passed to the local or global tables programmatically.

If the varPolicyNumber is the variable which holds the policy number which needs to be sent to the data table we can send that value into local sheet using the following statements into the Policy_Number column in the local sheet of the action.

varPolicyNumber = "123456"

DataTable("Policy_Number",dtLocalSheet) = varPolicyNumber

Working with External Excel sheets:

To send the data to the external excel file:

We have to define the automation objects to work with external excel file.

Set ExcelObj = CreateObject("Excel.Application")

The above line creates an Excel object ExcelObj which has reference to open excel file.

ExcelObj.Workbooks.Open "C:\Data\OutPut.xls"

Above statement opens the excel file "C:\Data\OutPut.xls" in the background.

Set NewSheet = ExcelObj.Sheets.Item("MyOutputSheet")

The above statement creates a sheet called "MyOutputSheet"

NewSheet.Cells(2,1) = VariableName

The above statement will populate the value present in the VariableName variable to the second row and first column of the sheet "MyOutputSheet".

Note: *The first row should be used for the row headers.*

ExcelObj.ActiveWorkbook.Save

The above statement saves the Excel file

ExcelObj.Application.Quit

The above statement quits or closes the Excel application.

Set ExcelObj = Nothing

The above statement nullifies the object ExcelObj.

To Delete the rows from external Excel sheet:

These statements open a excel sheet in the background and delete the rows 2 to 21.

```
Set ExcelObj = CreateObject("Excel.Application")
  ExcelObj.Workbooks.Open("C:\Deletetest.xls")
For i=1 to 20
  ExcelObj.Rows("2:21").Select
  ExcelObj.Selection.Delete
Next
    ExcelObj.ActiveWorkbook.Save
  ExcelObj.Application.Quit
  Set ExcelObj = Nothing
```

To Delete the rows from external Excel sheet from a specified sheet:

In this example the sheet name is DeleteSheet

```
Set ExcelObj = CreateObject("Excel.Application")
  ExcelObj.Workbooks.Open("C:\Deletetest.xls")
For i=1 to 20
  ExcelObj.Sheets("DeleteSheet").Rows("2:20").Select
  ExcelObj.Selection.Delete
```

```
Next
    ExcelObj.ActiveWorkbook.Save
  ExcelObj.Application.Quit
  Set ExcelObj = Nothing
```

1.9. Relative Path:

What is relative path and what are the advantages of it? How can you implement the relative path?

Relative path is a way of instructing QTP to search for the resources like Actions, Repositories, Function Libraries and Data Tables by just specifying the name of the resource. This is a very useful and powerful feature of QTP and can save weeks of operational time when the project has to be migrated to a different place from the existing drive. For example you developed all the scripts in the shared drive on the network and now your department bought TestDirector or QualityCenter and ask you to migrate all the scripts into TestDirector or QualityCenter. In the normal path or absolute path we go to the resources tab in the Test Settings and browse the resources for that script or action. If you have to change the location of the scripts you have to open each script and change the pointers to the resources in the resource tab. This could take from days to weeks depending on the number of scripts you have. The worst part is when you have a flow where you have calls to the reusable actions following the absolute path, you will have to build the whole new flow to replace the existing flow. On the other side if you have followed the relative path it is a one step process and could take not more than 10 minutes to change the resources. So question is how to implement the relative path mechanism.

Go to the Options from Tools menu and select Folders tab. Click on the green "+" sign in the search list section. Now browse the folders one by one where you store the actions, function libraries, data tables, object repositories, environment variables etc. Now whenever you are making calls to the resources just give the resource name excluding the path. QTP will search the search list folders for the resource specified and find the resource. When you migrate from one location to the other, you just have to go the folders tab in Options and delete the old folders and enter the new folders where your resources are residing.

Note:

Make sure that when you are using the relative path to call the resources, you are not duplicating the action names or repository names etc. If you have same names for the two resources, say for example: you have two projects with a shared object repository for each of them and you have name of the repository as "SharedObjectRepository" for both, when QTP searches the search folders specified in the options →folders it takes the first instance of the "SharedObjectRepository" in its path irrespective of the project. So you might end up calling the wrong shared object repository.
These settings effect the QTP settings and are not limited to the test or action you are working on.

Snapshot of the Folders Node to set the relative path.

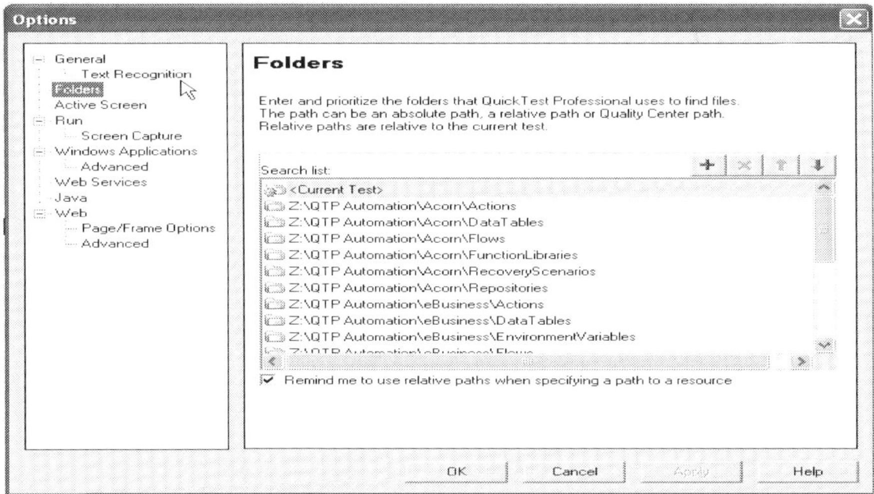

Note: In Version 10, check the checkbox: "Remind me to use relative paths when specifying a path to resource" in the Folders node of the options window. This will display a pop-up message when someone uses absolute path for calling the resources and by clicking "Yes" it is automatically changed to relative path and the folder is automatically added to the search folders list.

Please see the image below:

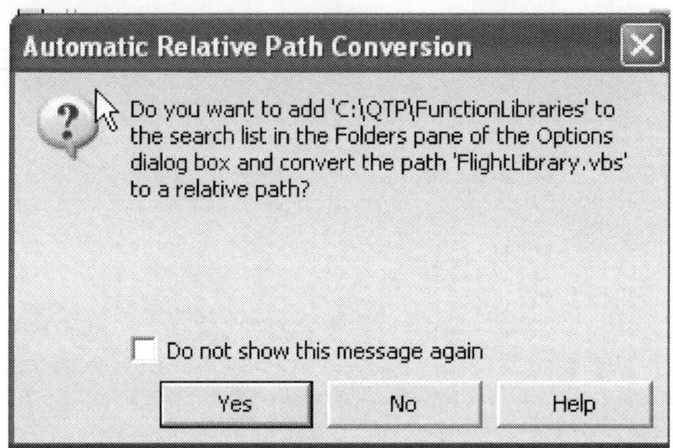

What is Regular Expression? How do you implement it?

When you have an object in your application whose properties keep changing dynamically based on the state of the application, we need to manage these objects using the regular expressions.

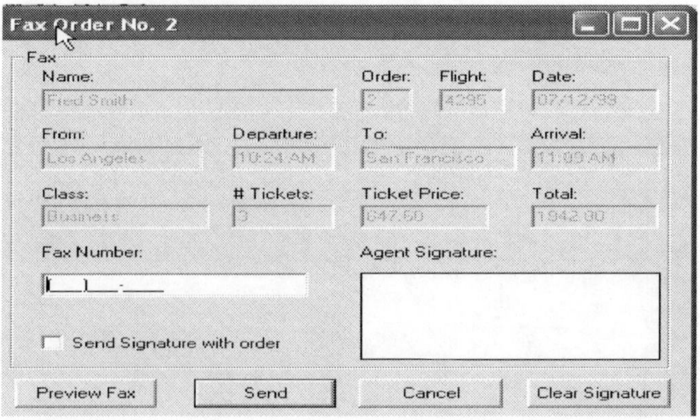

In the picture above the Fax order window has a title as “Fax Order No. 2” and for the next order it would have a title of “Fax Order No. 3” and so on and so forth. The window title is programmed to get the order number dynamically from the database and append to the words “Flight Order No.”. In this case we need to use a regular expression on the title property of this window in the object repository.

Open the object repository and locate this window. Then select the property (in this case it is “regexpwndtitle”). A little <#> sign appears in that field. Click on that and “Value Configurations Options” window opens showing the current value in the constant field. Select the checkbox “Regular Expression”. In the constant edit box enter the value “Fax Order.*” which indicates that whichever object has a title of “Fax Order” as the starting words will be recognized now irrespective of the numbers following. Here . (dot) represents one character and * (star) represents any number of characters or numbers.

Note: Once you click the checkbox “Regular Expression” you may get a popup asking you whether to add “\” to the value. Answer that with “No”. In QTP “\” has special meaning which can be like “\t” for tab, “\n” for newline character etc, and if we have to have a “\” in the value you want to pass as a regular expression you need to add one more “\” in front of it so that QTP is instructed not top consider the “\” as a special character but treat it as just a literal.

What is Active Screen and what are the advantages of it?

Active Screen is the snapshot of the application captured by QTP as it records on each object in the application. It shows the screen object corresponding to the script line where the cursor is currently positioned. This will help us in debugging the script. The Active Screen can also be used to put checkpoints in the script to check the functionality of the application.

1.10. Checkpoints:

What are checkpoints and how do you implement them?

Checkpoints are the verification points you insert to validate a particular part of the application.

1.10.1. Types of Checkpoints:

There are 8 types of checkpoints we can implement in QTP.

1. Standard Checkpoint
2. Text Checkpoint
3. Text Area Checkpoint
4. Bitmap Checkpoint
5. Database Checkpoint
6. Accessibility Checkpoint
7. XML Checkpoint (From Application)
8. XML Checkpoint (From Resource)

Here is the snapshot of the Checkpoints we can use in QTP.

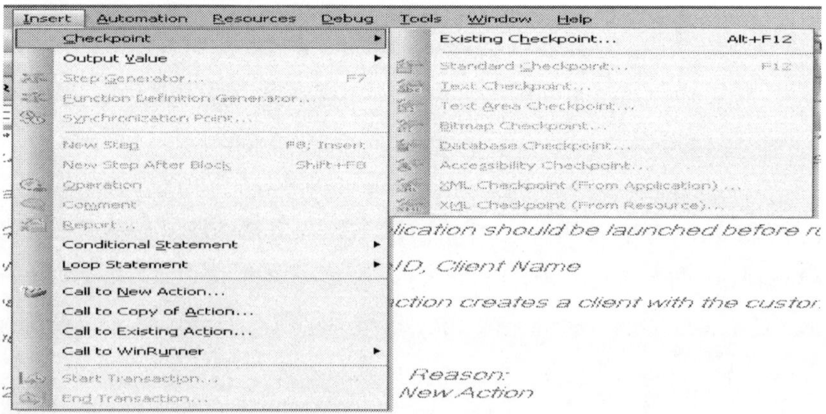

Checkpoints can be implemented in two ways:

Using Active Screen:

1.10.2. Standard Checkpoint:

Select the object from the Active Screen on which you need a checkpoint and right click. You will see a menu.

Select Insert Standard Checkpoint. You will be getting to the next screen showing the object in the tree view. Select the object from the tree and you will go to the Checkpoint Properties window.

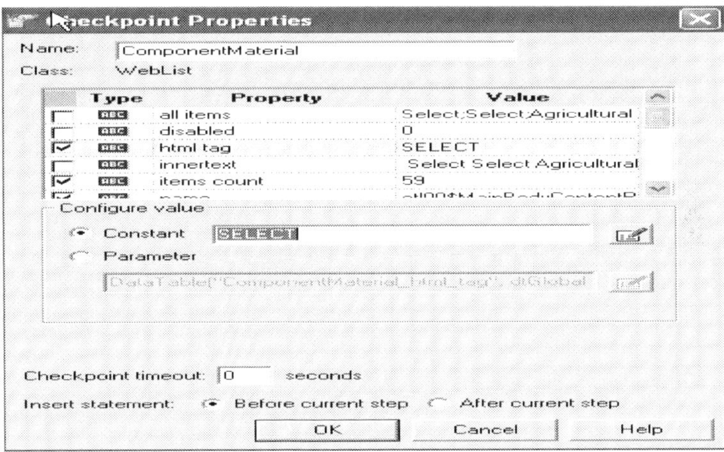

From this window select the properties you want to be checked every time you run the script. Each property can be either hard coded (i.e. leave the existing value as the expected result) or can be parameterized from the data table value or you can specify a regular expression for that property.

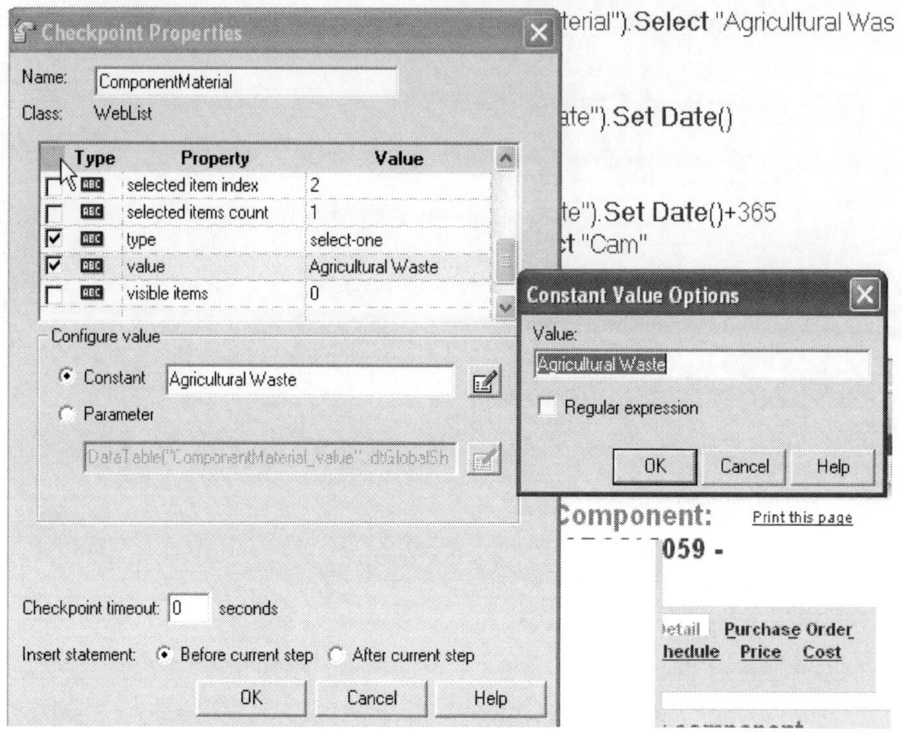

1.10.3. Recording checkpoints on live application:

To record the checkpoint on the running application you should start the record session and select Insert Checkpoint → Standard checkpoint from the Insert menu. Then point the hand icon to the part of the application on which you want to insert the checkpoint.

1.10.4. Text Checkpoint:

When you want to check if a specified text is displayed or even not displayed on the application screen we can use Text Checkpoint. For example if you want to verify that the "Flight Details" heading is displayed everytime you run the regression test you can do that while in the record mode. Select

"Insert"→Checkpoint→ Text Checkpoint and point the hand icon to the text you want to verify. Text Checkpoint Properties window will open and it displays the text you clicked on in red which indicates that the verification will be done for that text and the drop down will have the "Checked Text" selected.

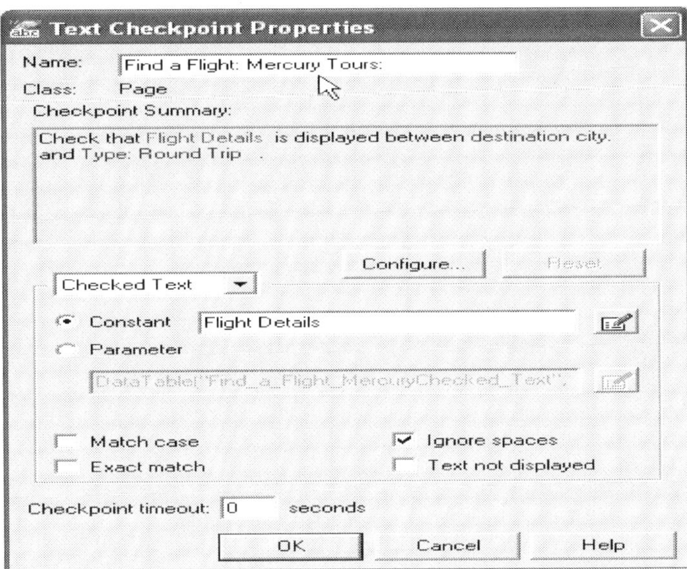

You can configure the text before and text after the Checked Text if you need to. Click on the "Configure" button and highlight the text you want as the text which should appear before the actual text you are verifying and click Text before and do the same for Text After the actual text. Click "OK" to close the "Configure Text Selection" window and click "OK" on "Text Checkpoint Properties" window to finalize and insert the checkpoint.

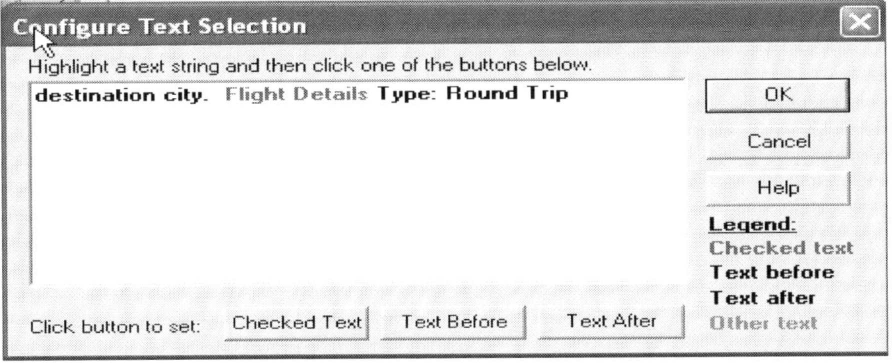

You can also parameterize the text checkpoint by clicking on the Parameter radio button and selecting the data table field from which you want to drive the checkpoint data or you can also give regular expression to the checkpoint by clicking on the "pencil" icon beside the Constant field and specifying the regular expression pattern after checking the checkbox "Regular Expression" in the Constant Value Options window.

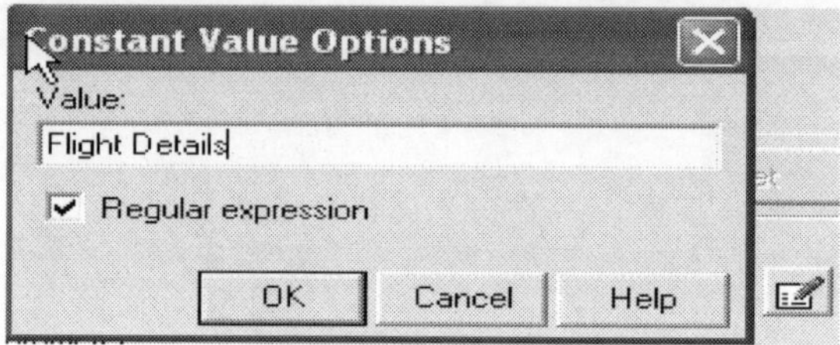

1.10.5. Bitmap Checkpoint:

Bitmap checkpoints can be used when you want to verify that an image appears on the screen (Example; Logo of the company). Bitmap checkpoints depend very closely on the screen resolution and can fail even when there is slight variation in the screen resolution. For example if you record the checkpoint on a laptop and try to run the same script on a desktop you might see a failure in the bitmap checkpoint. I strongly recommend avoiding bitmap checkpoints and instead write a function to verify the images using the .Exist method on the image you want to verify which should return "True" when the object exists and "False" when object does not exist.

To create a Bitmap Checkpoint, start recording and select Insert→Checkpoint→Bitmap Checkpoint and point the cursor to the image you want to check. Bitmap Checkpoint Properties window comes up. You can rename the checkpoint by changing the name in QTP 9 and above versions but you can't change the name in 8.2. Click on the "Select Area…" button and the cursor turns into a cross. Select the area of the image you want to verify. Once you do that the checkbox "Save only selected area" gets highlighted. Check that checkbox. You will get a popup saying that only the portion you selected will be saved in the checkpoint. Accept it by clicking "Yes". Click "OK" to create the checkpoint.

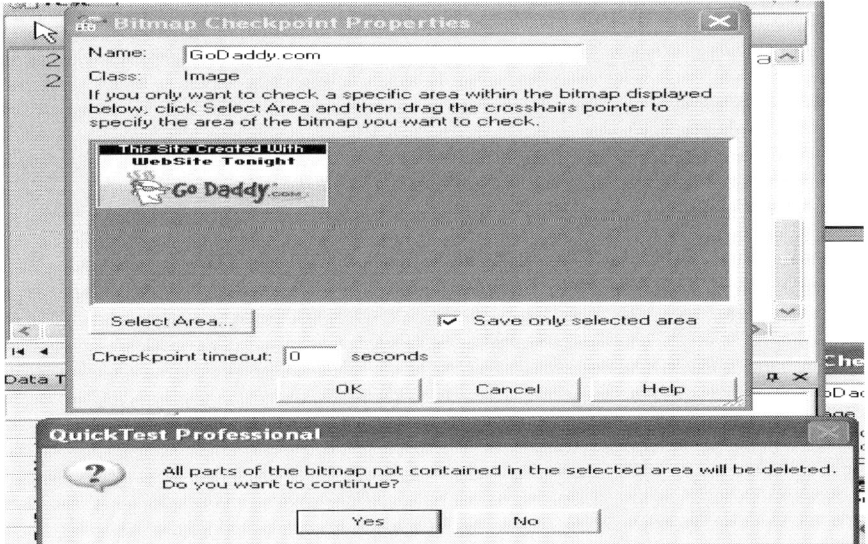

Note: For every checkpoint you can specify the extra timeout you want to specify in addition to the 10 seconds timeout which QTP settings come with.

1.10.6. Database Checkpoint:

Database checkpoint can be used if you want to verify that the data you want to verify (expected result) exists in the database as expected. When you create a database checkpoint you should specify the SQL query which fetches the data you want to store in the checkpoint as the expected result and when you run the checkpoint QTP will check the database values using the stored SQL query in the checkpoint against the stored values in the checkpoint.

To insert the database checkpoint select Insert → Checkpoint →Database Checkpoint.

You will see a Database Query Wizard window which will guide you through the process of creating a database checkpoint. Check the Radio button

“Specify SQL statement manually’ to enter the SQL query in the next screen. Select the checkbox beside “Maximum number of rows” and enter the number of rows you want to extract for the query you specify in the checkpoint. This step is optional but if the database is large and has millions or thousands of records you might want to extract only a limited number of rows. Click “Next”.

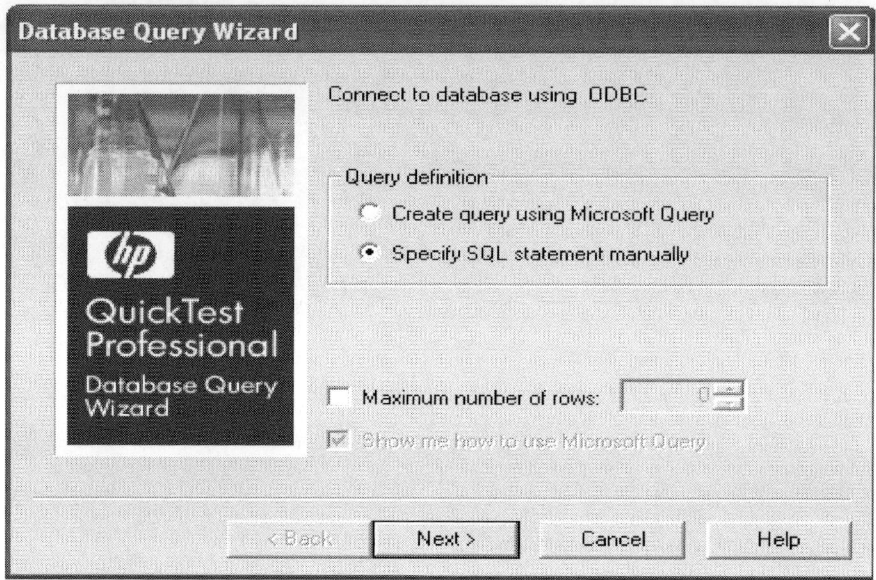

The next screen will have the sections to specify the Connection string and SQL Statement. Connection string is a way of instructing QTP about the database you want to connect to extract the data.

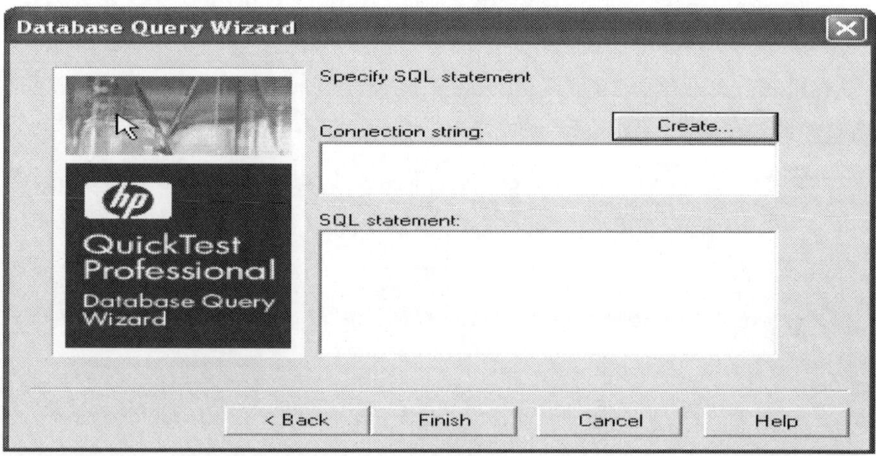

Click on the button “Create” and you will get the “Select Data Source” window.

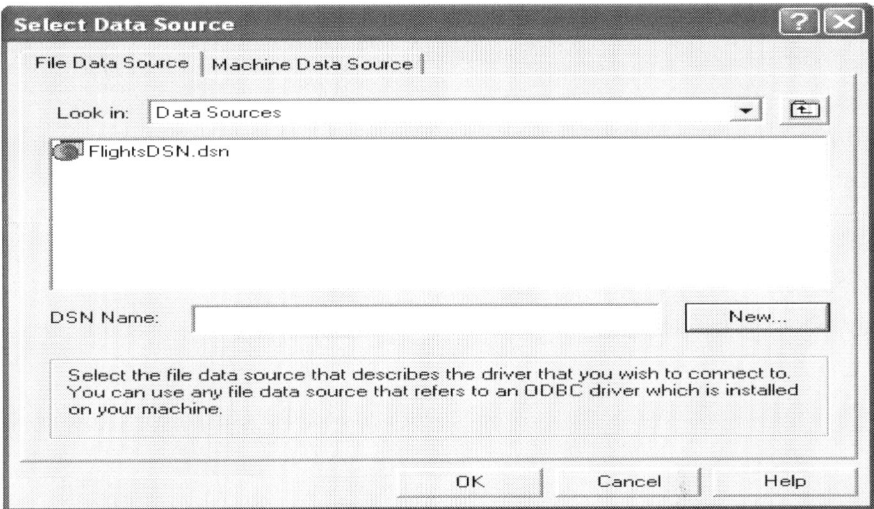

In this window you can select the data source which is already defined in that machine or if it is not listed you can create a new one by clicking “New”. Click “New” button. “Create New Data Source” window opens up listing all the database drivers. Select the database driver which suits your database and click “Next”.

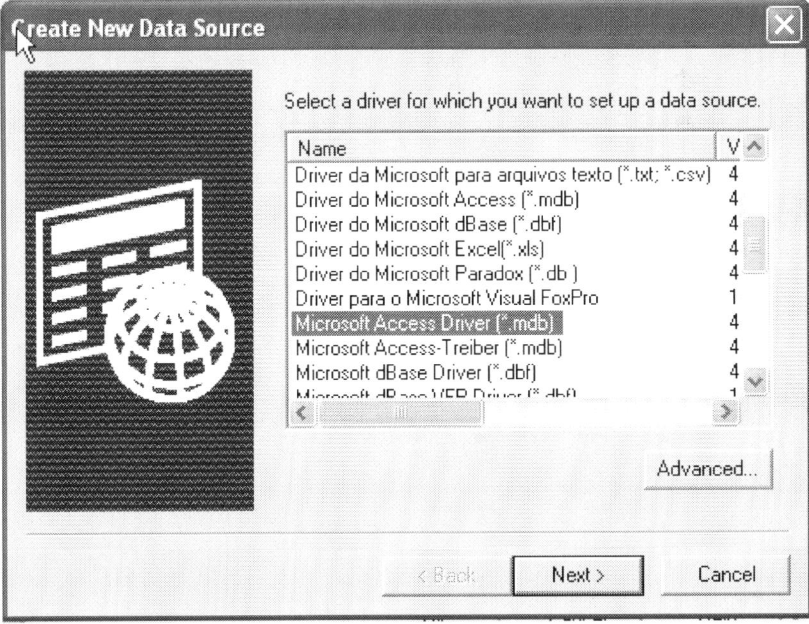

In the next screen give the relevant file name which will be your new Data source Name (DSN) and click "Next".

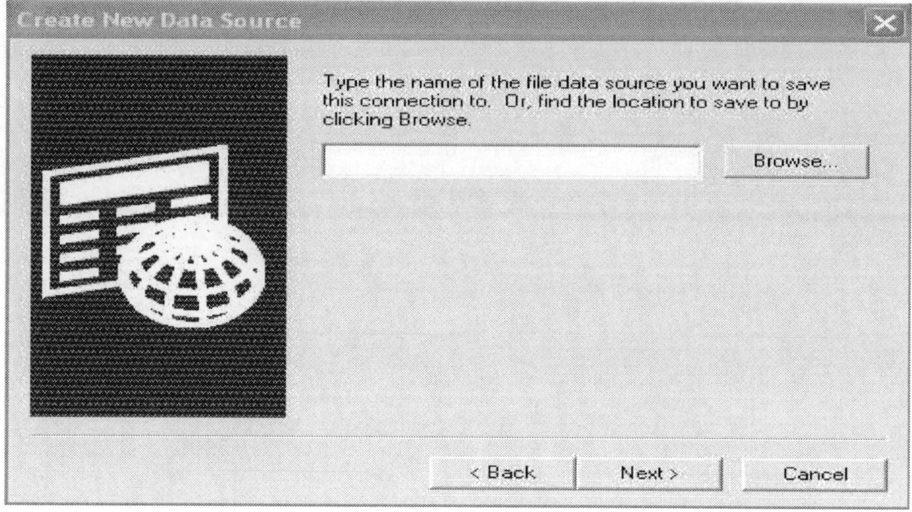

On the next screen Click "Finish". "ODBC Microsoft Access Setup" window opens. The window title changes with the database you are connecting to.

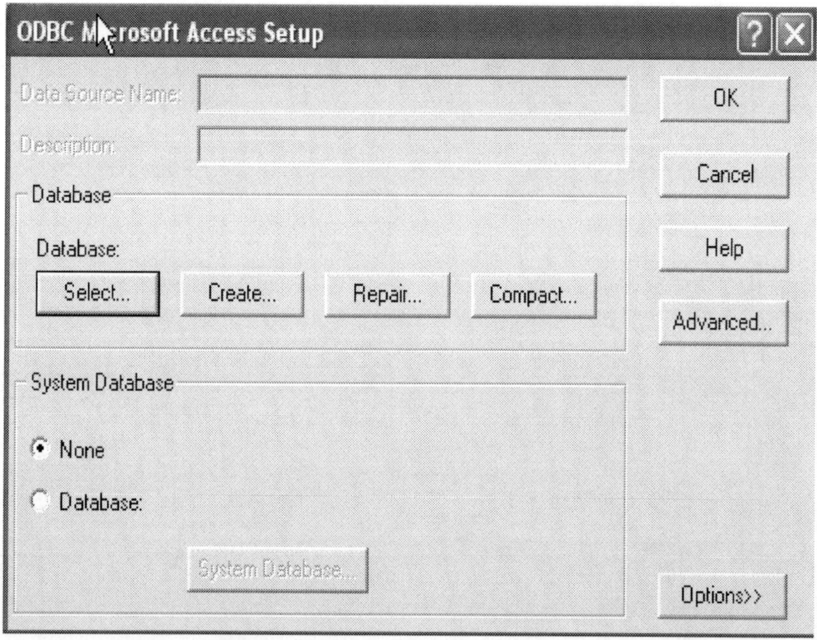

In this screen you need to select the actual database name to which you to connect to. Click on "Select' and "Select Database" window opens.

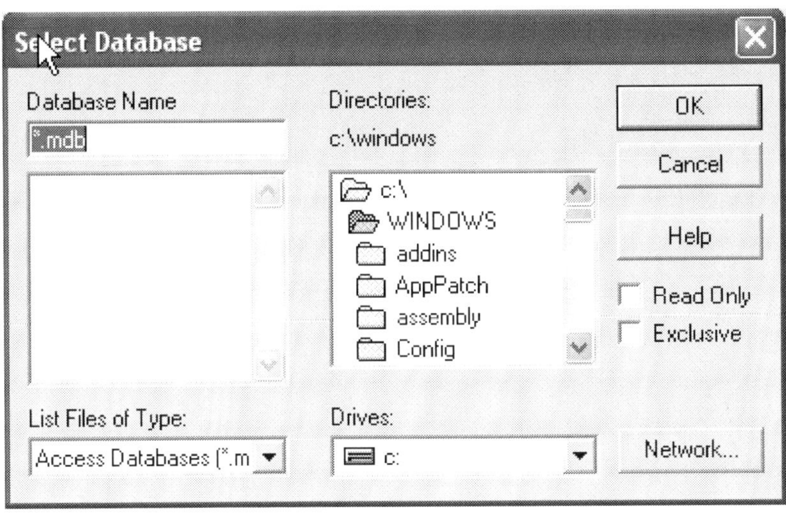

Browse through the network to find the database file which acts as your database and click “OK”. Click “OK” to close the “ODBC Microsoft Access Setup” window. You will be taken back to the “Select Data Source” window where the name which you specified for the DSN can be seen and it is selected. Click “OK” to close the window and the Connection string section of the “Database Query Wizard” will be populated with the connection string which has all the information you specified in the earlier steps. Enter the SQL query in the SQL Statement section and click “Finish”.

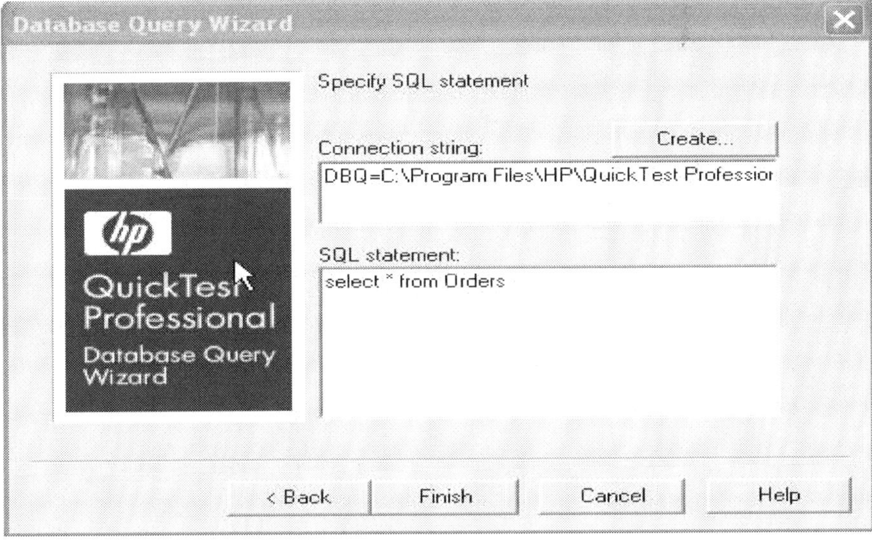

Database Checkpoint properties window opens up with the data resulting from the query you specified.

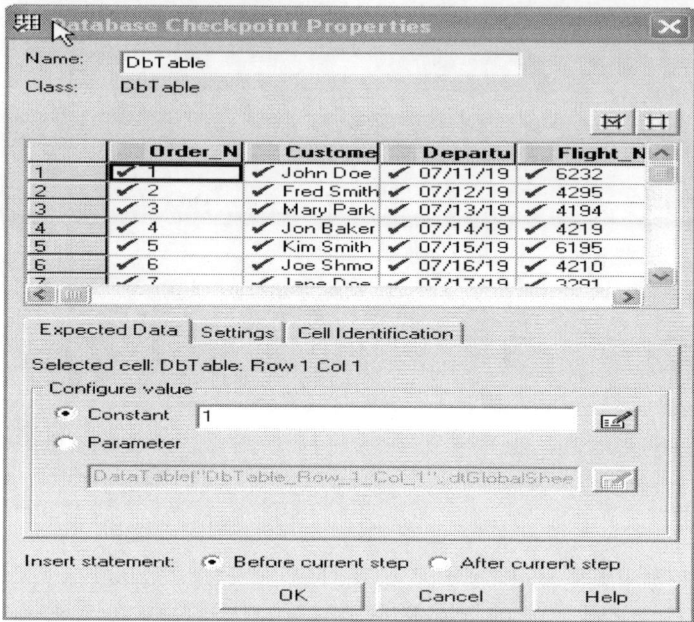

You can leave the data as it is if the data should always be static or you can parameterize the data if you want by clicking on the “Paramater” radio button and specifying the table column for each cell.

By default all the data cells are marked for check but if you want to deselect some of them you can use the following buttons by selecting each cell in the checkpoint. The first icon starts for “Add to check” and the second one stands for “Remove from check”.

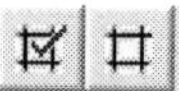

Click “OK” to insert the checkpoint. The statement “DbTable("DbTable").Check CheckPoint("DbTable")” is inserted one line above cursor position if you selected the Radio button “Before current step” or one line below your cursor position if you selected the option “After current step”.

1.10.7. Accessibility Checkpoint:

Accessibility Checkpoint is used to find out if the application coding standards meet and follow the standard set forth by W3C (World Wide Web Consortium).

By default this checkpoint is configured to check only for the Alt tag property check for each object referenced in the application.

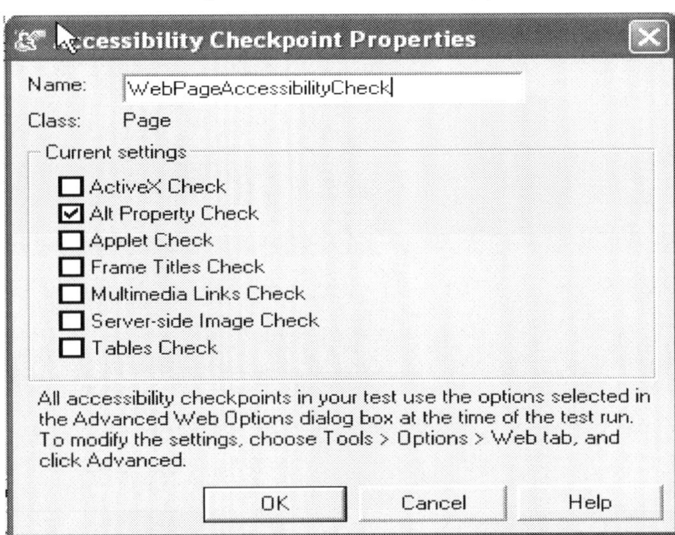

In order to configure the checkpoint to check other standards and checks on a web page, go to Tools →Options menu, click on Web tab and then click on the button “Advanced”. You will get the “Advanced Web Options” window.

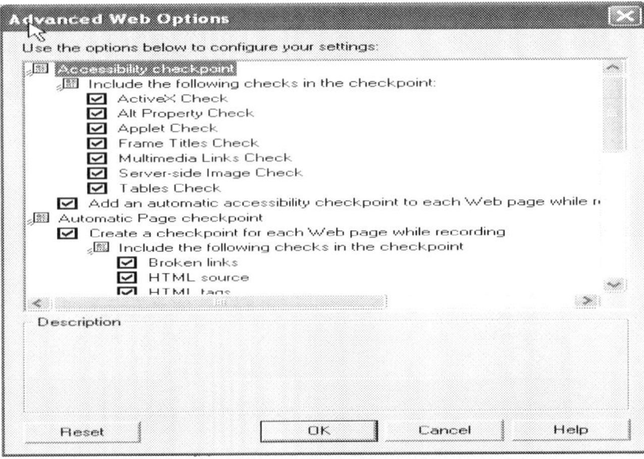

Select the various attributes you would like to be included in the Accessibility Checkpoint, by checking the checkboxes beside each Check under Accessibility checkpoint section of the window. Then click OK to close the window and click OK to close the Options window.

Now you can insert the Accessibility checkpoint by starting record session and going to Insert →Checkpoint and selecting Accessibility Checkpoint. Then point the web page you want the checkpoint on.

1.10.8. XML Checkpoint (From Application):

XML Checkpoint (From Application) is a way of recording the checkpoint on the application which is XML based to verify that the XML values are properly displayed on the screen. Open the application which is XML based and start recording and select Insert →Checkpoint→XML Checkpoint (From Application) and point the hand to the XML based web application. QTP will capture all the XML tags and values along with their child elements and stores as the properties. You can uncheck the attributes or node values which you do not want to include in the checkpoint. Also you can specify the level of checking the child elements by incrementing the number under the checkbox “Check number of child element occurrences in block” after checking the checkbox.

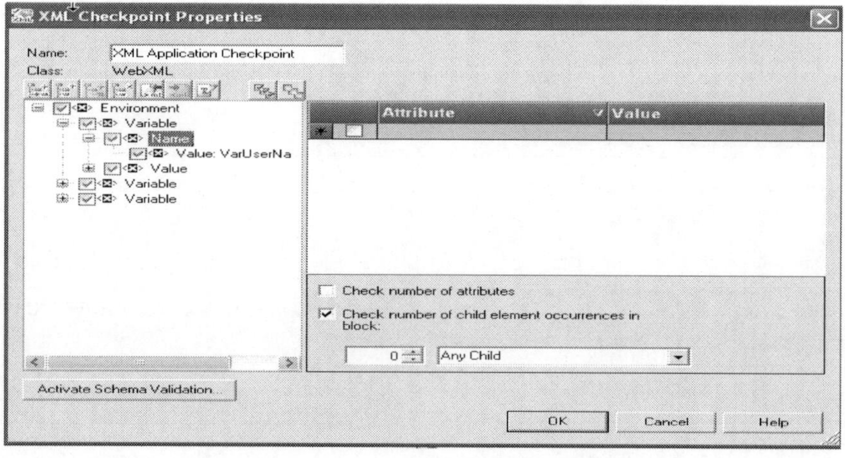

Since almost all applications being build these days are XML based applications, this is a powerful feature QTP provides us to validate that the data is consistently displayed every time a new build is given to QA team.

We can also parameterize the checkpoint properties by clicking on the value attribute of each node. Click on the <#> sign in the value field and you will get the Value Configuration Options window where you can either select the data from the data table or use a regular expression.

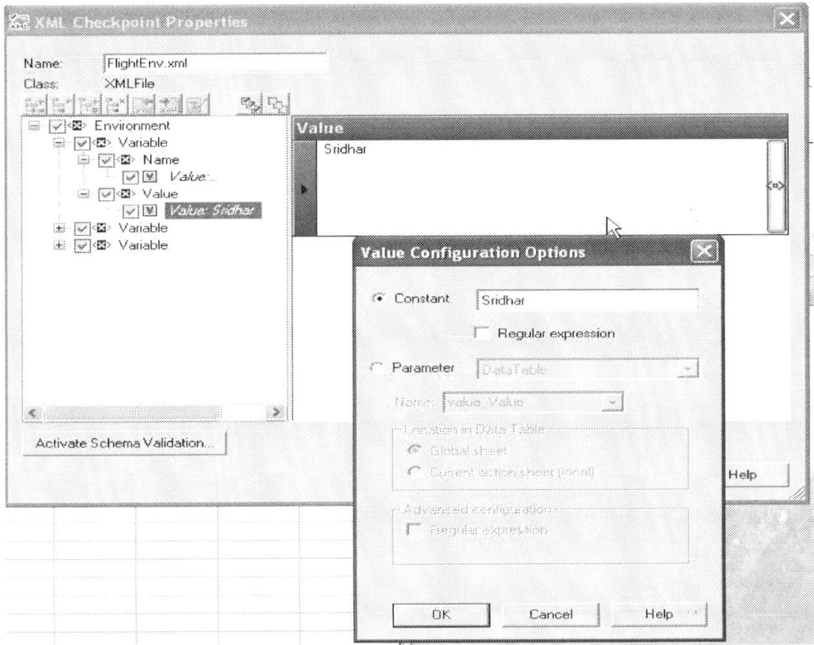

1.10.9. XML Checkpoint (From Resource):

You can check the contents of an XML file using this checkpoint. This can be recorded even when you are not in the record mode. Once you select to insert this checkpoint XML Source Selection box comes up.

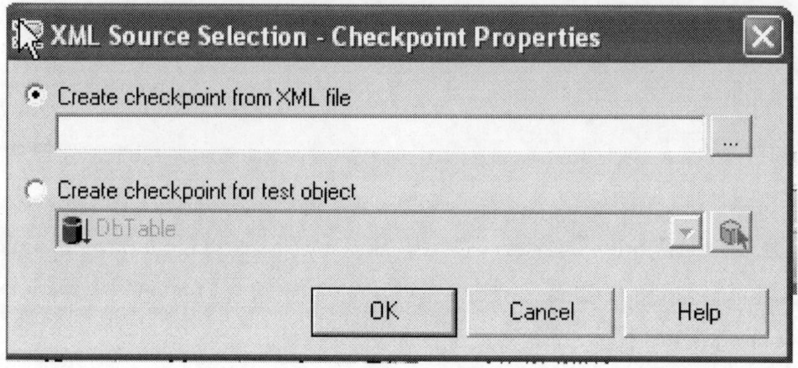

You can browse the folders and select the XML file on which you want this checkpoint. This checkpoint verifies that the XML file has the same nodes and values both while recording the checkpoint and when when it is played back. Variations in the XML source may cause the display problems in the application which is actually using these resource files and hence checking for consistency of the XML source file is very important for checking the XML based applications.

1.11. Recovery Scenarios:

What is a Recovery Scenario and how do you implement it?

Recovery Scenario is where QTP handles any unexpected windows, pop-ups or application crashes while the test is running so that the test is not interrupted. Each type of recovery situation should be handled with a separate recovery scenario. These recovery scenarios will be constantly looking for the recovery situations occurring in the application as long as the test is running.
To create a recovery scenario: Select “recovery Scenario Manager” from the “Resources” menu.

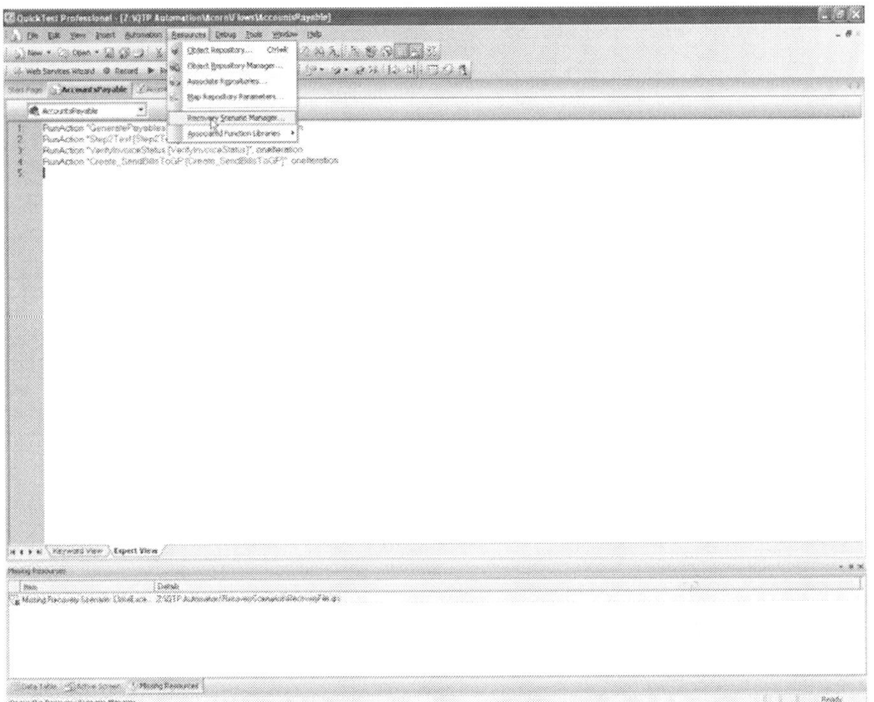

Recovery Scenario Wizards starts. Click Next on this screen.

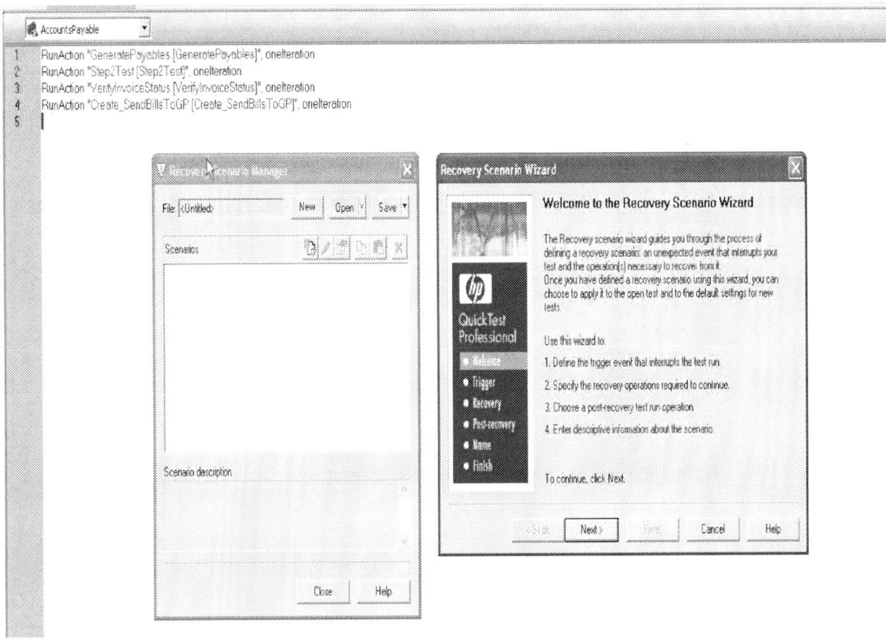

Depending on what type of recovery scenario you want to define, select the appropriate Radio button. We can define the recovery scenarios for unwanted Pop-up window, Object state, Test run error or application crash.

Recovery Scenario Wizard

Select Trigger Event

Select the trigger event type that will trigger the recovery operation.

- Pop-up window
  A window pops up in an opened application during the test run.
- Object state
  The property values of an object in your application match specified values. You can specify property values for each object in the hierarchy.
- Test run error
  A step in your test does not run successfully.
- Application crash
  An open application fails during the test run.

QuickTest Professional

- Welcome
- Trigger
- Recovery
- Post-recovery
- Name
- Finish

< Back | Next > | Finish | Cancel | Help

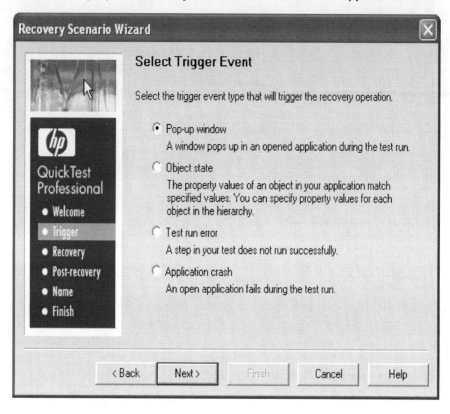

Click Next button and show the pop-up window.

An example Pop-up window is show below which appears when navigating from non-secure to secure web page.

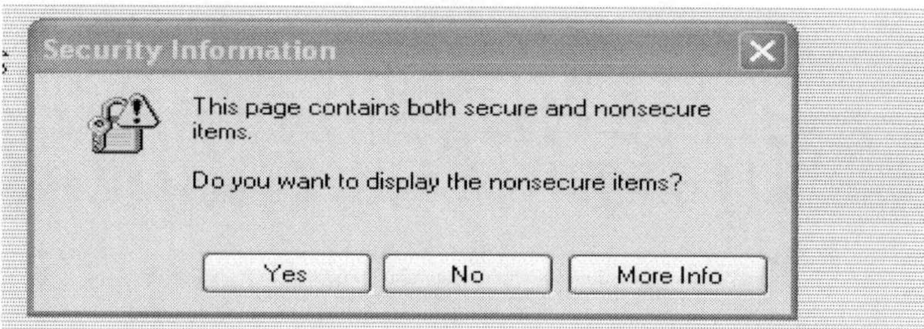

QTP captures the window title and window text. Uncheck the checkbox which says "Window text contains". This makes QTP look for any security window with the title Security Information or any generic title. If the window title changes dynamically with some pattern check the checkbox "Regular Expression" and provide the pattern. Click Next.

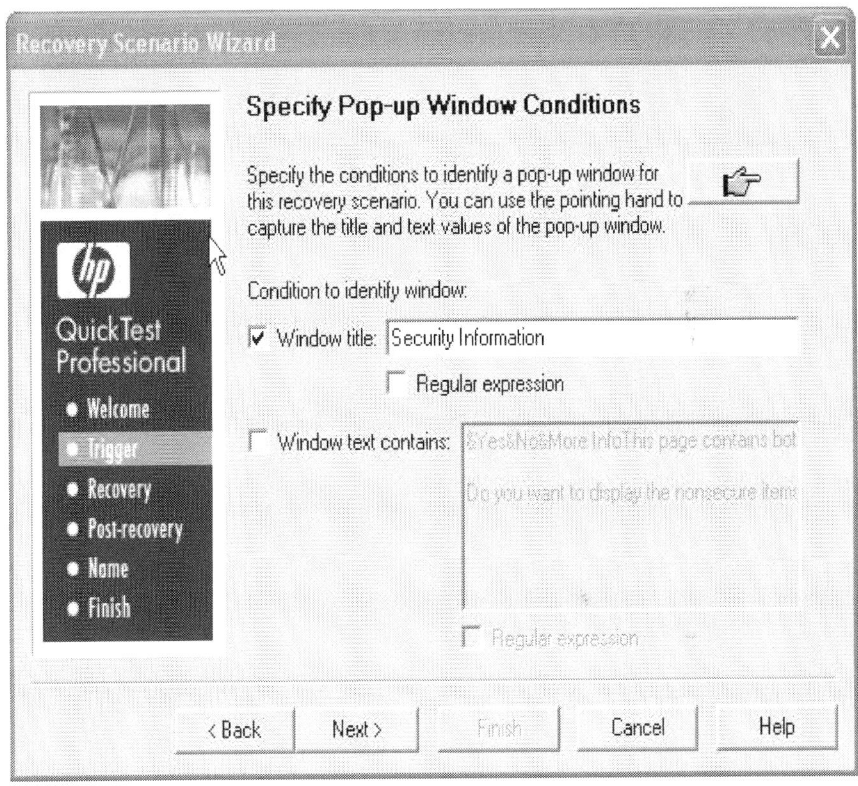

Next screen informs that you should define the recovery operation to be done in order to handle this window.

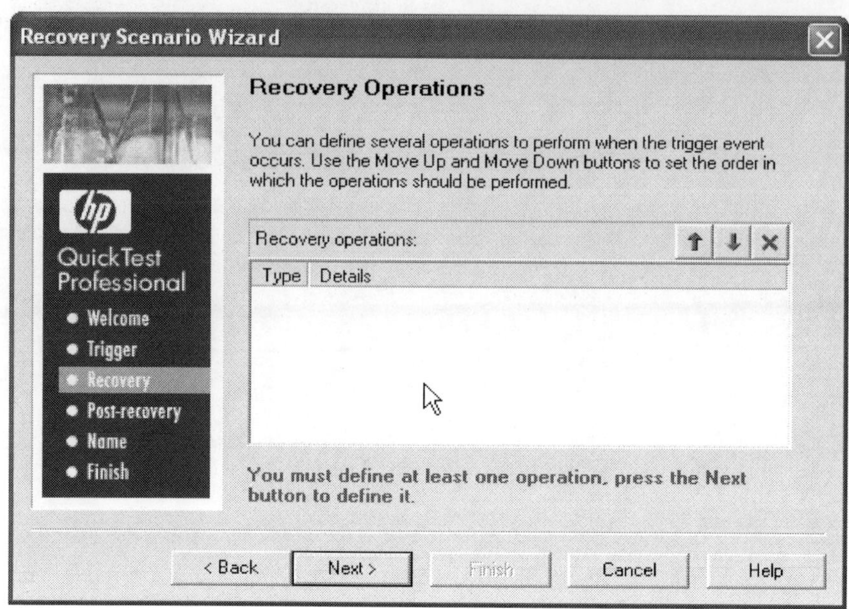

Click next button and you will be taken to Recovery Operation window. You can select the appropriate action to be performed.

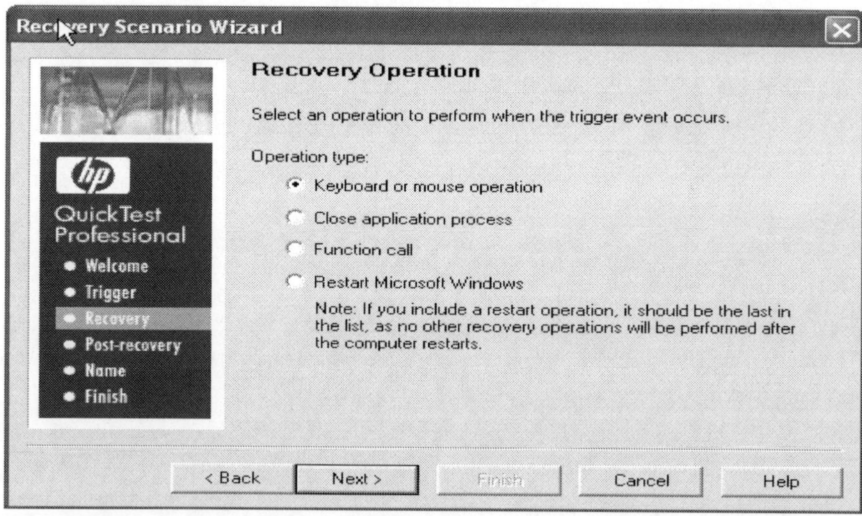

Keyboard or mouse operation allows us to click a button on the screen.

Close application process allows us to kill the process which starts the unwanted window so we can continue with testing.

Function call will allow us to write a user-defined function to handle the un-wanted window.

Restart Microsoft Windows allows us to restart the windows all together if needed.

For this above example, click on the first radio button “Keyboard or mouse operation”. You can show the button you want QTP to click using the hand icon in the next screen and click Next button.

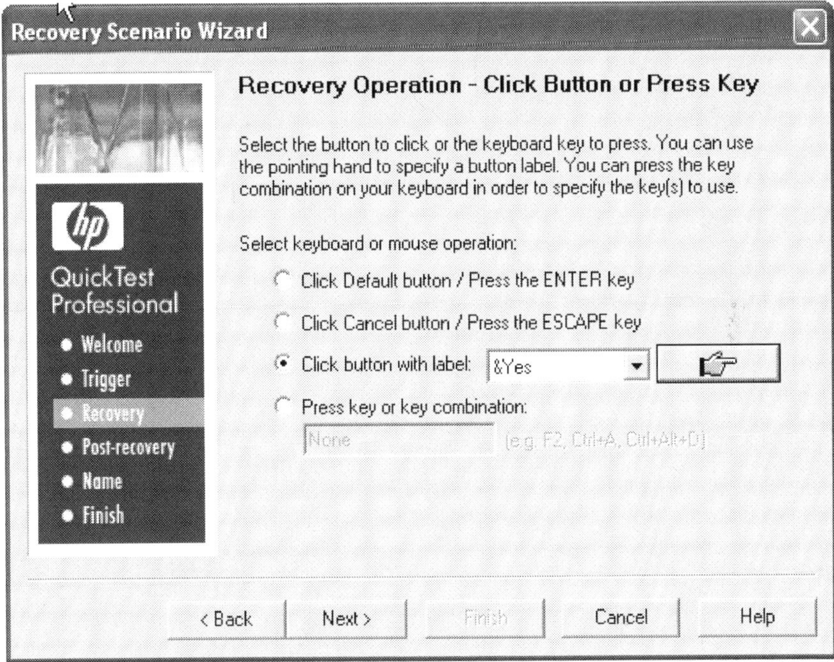

You can add another recovery scenario if needed from the below screen. If you don’t want to create another scenario uncheck the checkbox “Add another recovery operation” and click “Next”.

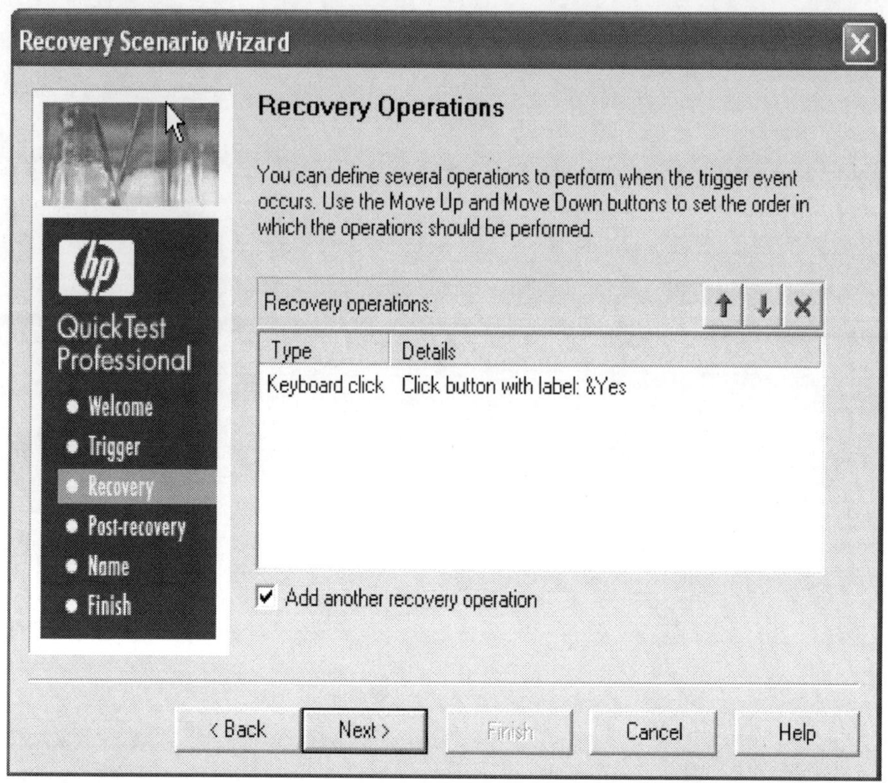

Next screen will allow us to define the Post-recovery operation to be performed. Since the recovery scenario is kicked off only when the error is about to be thrown since QTP could not find an object because of the unwanted window or object state it makes sense to re-execute that statement again after the post-recovery operation. So select the option “Repeat current step and continue”. If that is not the situation make the appropriate selection depending on the operation you want to make. If the exception does not allow us to test the application anymore in this test run select the last radio button “Stop the test run”

Use proceed to next step if you want to continue with the test.

Use proceed to next action if you want to skip the current action in the flow and continue with the next action.

Use Proceed to next test iteration if you want to skip the current row of global row and continue with the next row of Global sheet.

Use Restart current test run if you want to start the test altogether.

Click Next.

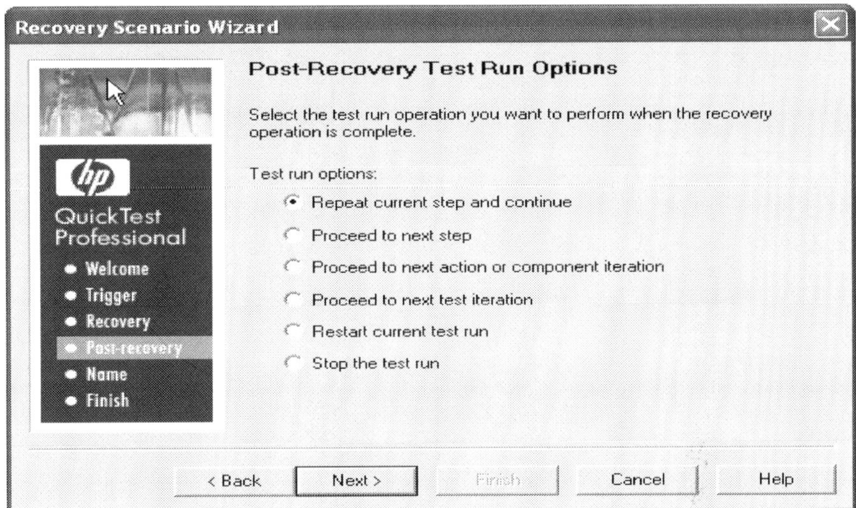

Give the name to the recovery scenario and click “Next”.

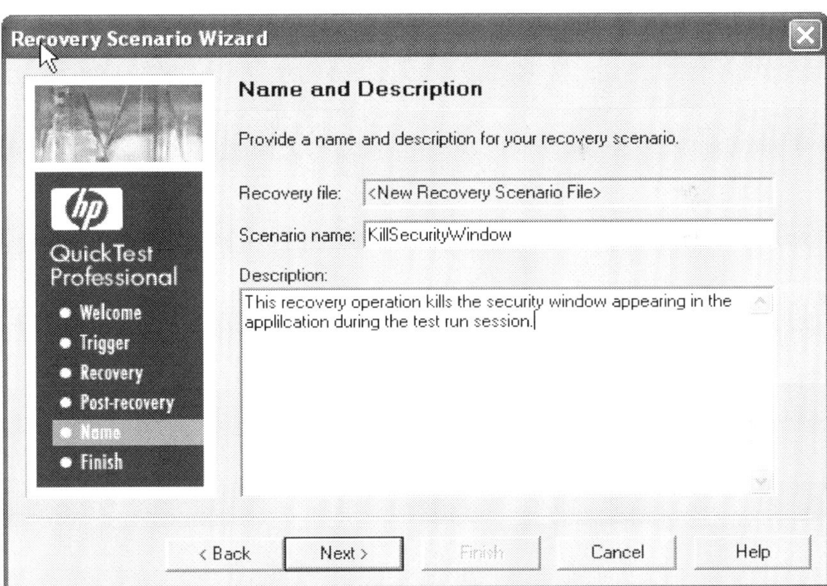

Make sure that the checkboxes “Add scenario to current test” and “Add scenario to default test settings” are selected in order to add the Recovery scenario to the current and the QTP settings as well.

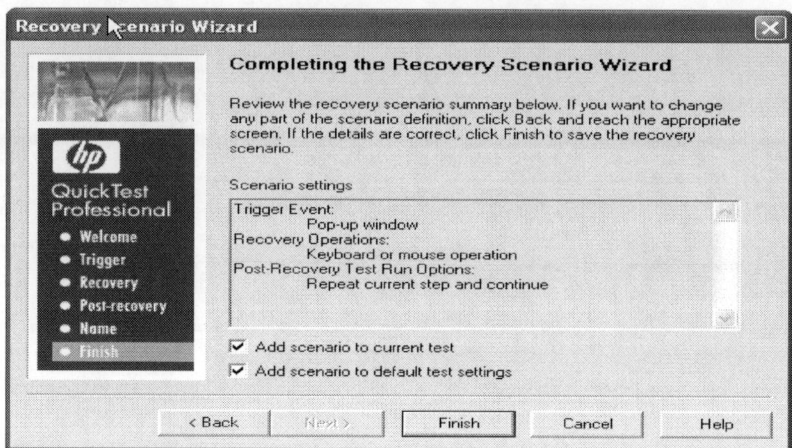

Click “Finish” and save the recovery scenario to a recovery file by hitting the save button in the next screen.

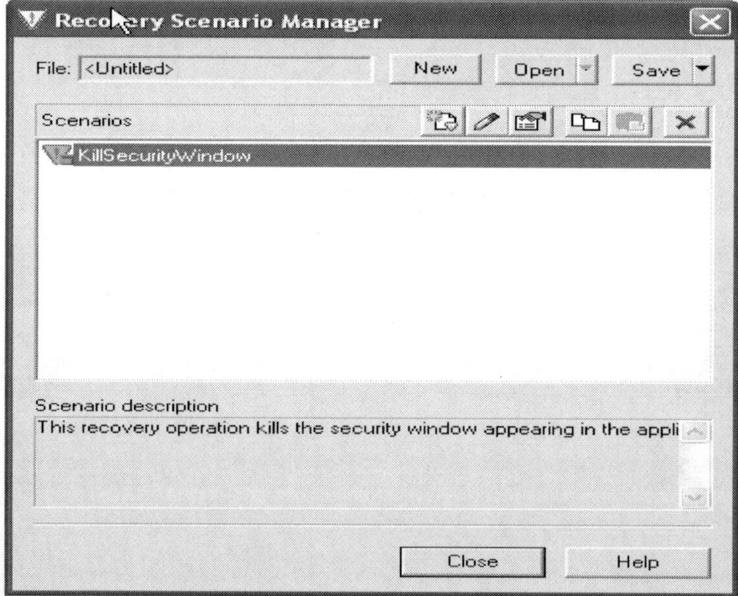

Save the file to the disk.

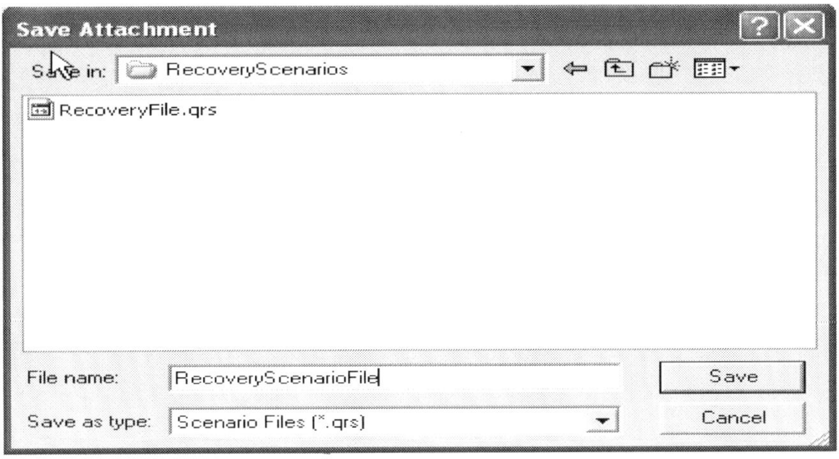

1.12. Keyword Driven Testing Framework:

Keyword Driven Testing is a convenient and easy way of developing the automation scripts by the less technical people like SME or Business Analyst.

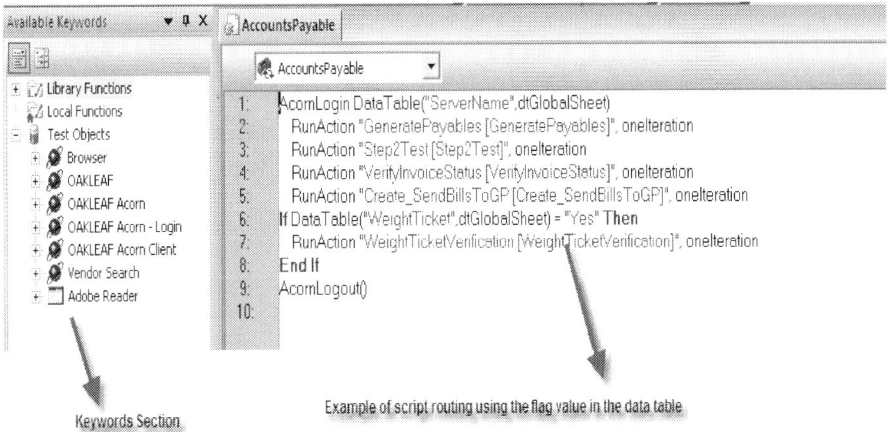

In this frame work each resource of QTP is considered as a Keyword and can be dragged and dropped into the script area from the “Available Keywords” section.

For being successful with this framework the names of the resources should be clear and precise to what that resource does. Example: a function which creates a Policy for a customer can be called as "CreatePolicy". As you expand the each folder in the Available Keywords section we see all the resources or Key words listed.

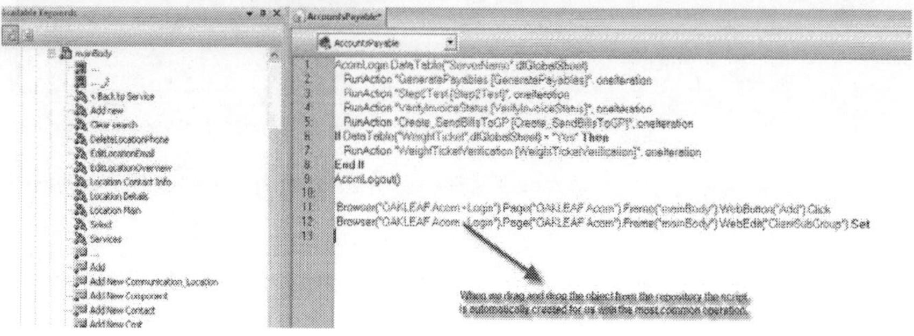

When you drag and drop the objects from the Object repository to the script area, the script is automatically populated for us with the most common method used for that kind of object.

Example:

Browser("OAKLEAF Acorn – Login").Page("OAKLEAF Acorn").Frame("mainBody").WebButton("Add").Click

Browser("OAKLEAF Acorn – Login").Page("OAKLEAF Acorn").Frame("mainBody").WebEdit("ClientSubGroup").Set

And when you do the same from Key Word view it even allows you to set the value for that method. In the example snapshot show below, the value of the Edit field "CommunicationValue" can be set by clicking in the "Value" field of the Keyword view for that object after dragging that object and by clicking "#" sign which opens the "Value Configuration Options" window where you can enter the value or parameterize the value.

The key to the success of the Key word driven framework is creating as many functions as possible for the application and adding all the objects of the application to the repository before starting the project.

There can be 2 types of function libraries. One for application specific library where we store all the functions which cover the test cases, and one with generic functions which includes the functions like CloseAllBrowsers(), VerifyObjectEnabled etc.

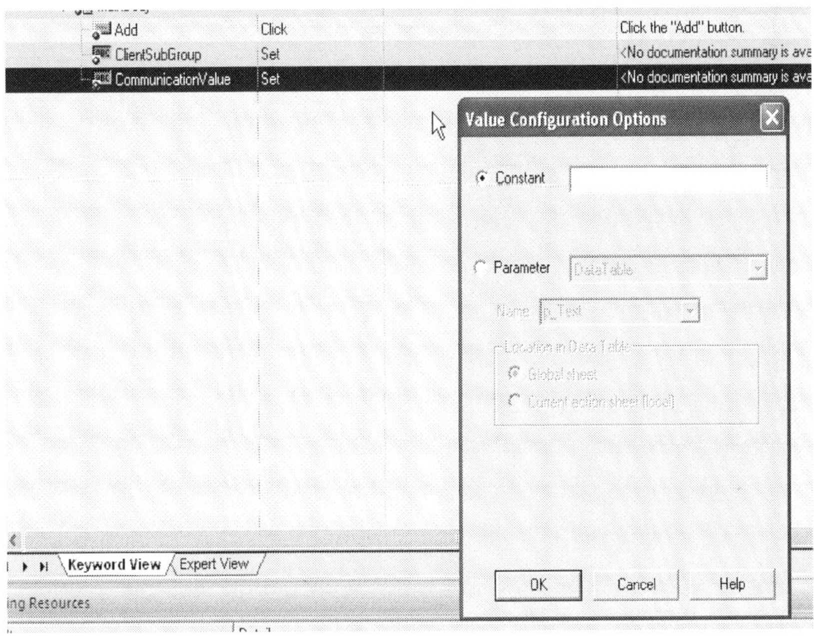

This Framework can be further made simple by using the Keywords or flags from the data table.

Example:

```
If DataTable("WeightTicket",dtGlobalSheet) = "Yes" Then
    RunAction "WeightTicketVerification [WeightTicketVerification]", oneIteration
End If
```

In the above example, the flag “WeightTicket” in the Global Sheet is set to “Yes” or “No” and depending on the value of that flag we eight run the Action pertaining to that functionality, in this case the action name is “WeightTicketVerification”.

The keyword frame work emphasizes that all the functionality is coded in the functions and these functions dragged into the script area and thus avoiding the script outside the function library and thus it is very important to name the functions carefully with relevant and meaningful name. If you use multiple function libraries, make sure the function names are not repeated and are unique.

There should be an Initialization script which loads all the required resources into QTP and that should be called in to the Driver script which has flow of actions (This driver script can be called as a Flow). The initialization script should be the first script in the flow of actions.

1.13. Script Debugging:

Script debugging is a process, where we go through the code line by line while executing the script and see what script is doing at every step. This will be helpful if we want to fix the script which is not performing the expected job. Debugging is a process of eliminating the bugs in our QTP scripts.
To start the debugging process, go to "Debug" menu and select the debug process you want to perform. You can start debugging from the current cursor position or you can run the script up to the cursor position in debug mode. There are two kinds of debugging processes again. If you choose "Step Into" you can see if a function you are executing is performing the expected job. This will open the function which you want to debug in "Read Only" mode and you can keep pressing the "F11" function key on the keyboard to see the execution of each line of the function. But, if you are sure that the function is working perfect and you don't want to see the execution of the function you can choose "Step Over" or hit "F10" function key which will execute the whole function without stopping and will stop for our next command at the beginning of the next line after the function call.

You can also watch the values of the variables by adding the variables to the watch list. To do this place the cursor on the variable whose value needs to be watched while the script is being executed and from the "Debug" menu, select "Add to Watch". You will see that variable added to the Watch list in the debug viewer at the bottom of the script.

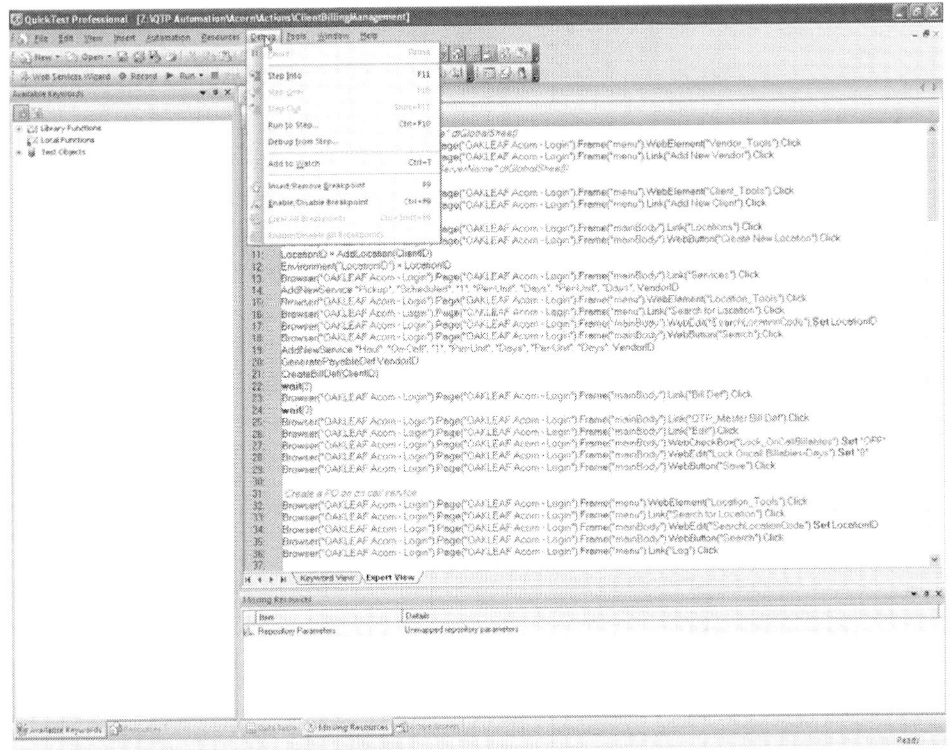

1.14. Interacting with Database using SQL queries

We can write the SQL queries and do the inserts, deletes and updates of the records in the database using QTP scripts if the situation demands.
We need the Data Source Name (DSN) information which we can create using the Database checkpoint. While creating the database checkpoint, once the DSN is created you can see the code for the connection from QTP to database. Copy this and save this string so you can use it when connecting directly from the script and not through the checkpoint. This DSN establishes the connection between QTP and the database you are trying to work on.

We can drive the input to the SQL query using the data table values. Here is an example QTP script which connects to the sample flight VB application's database which is provided with QTP and deletes the order from the Orders table taking the order number from the "OrderNumber" field in the Global Sheet of the data table.

```
Set MyConn = CreateObject ("ADODB.Connection")

MyConn.ConnectionString = "DBQ=C:\Program Files\HP\QuickTest
Professional\samples\flight\app\flight32.mdb;DefaultDir=C:\Program
Files\HP\QuickTest Professional\samples\flight\app;Driver={Microsoft Access Driver
(*.mdb, *.accdb)};DriverId=281;FIL=MS Access;FILEDSN=C:\Program Files\Common
Files\ODBC\Data
Sources\FlightJuly09DSN.dsn;MaxBufferSize=2048;MaxScanRows=8;PageTimeout=
5;SafeTransactions=0;Threads=3;UID=admin;UserCommitSync=Yes;"

Set RecordSet = CreateObject ("ADODB.Recordset")

RecordSet.CursorType = 1

OrderNumber=DataTable("OrderNumber", dtGlobalSheet)

SQLQuery="Delete Orders.Order_Number FROM Orders WHERE
Orders.Order_Number ="&OrderNumer

MyConn.Open

RecordSet.Open SQLQuery, MyConn

MyConn.Close

Set MyConn = Nothing
```

Key Concepts and Definitions

2.1. Action

b. An action is a QTP script used for testing a particular segment of the application. Actions help in dividing the tests into logical units. An action can be of two types, reusable and non-reusable.

c. If the functionality within an application is called by many different modules, then the process of testing that functionality should be made a re-usable action. For instance an action called "Submission Search" is used by more than one module. Therefore testing of this segment should be made into a reusable action.

2.2. Flow

a. Each reusable action will be called sequentially from a separate script. This script which calls all the actions pertaining to the business functionality sequentially is called a "Flow".

b. All the reusable actions and the flow should load the same add-ins. This can avoid long delays in launching the test flow.

2.3. Data Table

Data Table is an excel table which holds the data to be entered into the application to test the various conditions of business functionality.

It consists of two kinds of one Global sheet and one local sheet per action. Global sheet is used as an input sheet where all the data to be entered into the application across all the actions in the test flow should be entered in the global sheet. Each row of the global sheet indicates a separate test case.

Sometimes we take some values from the application for instance when a policy is issued to the customer, the policy number generated automatically by the application is to be used elsewhere in the automation process. These values which should be available across the actions should also be sent to the global sheet.

Local action sheet should have values which should be entered into the application only if for some reason we need to execute that action more than one iteration. Local sheet can also be used to store the output values being grabbed from the application for reporting purposes. If these output values have to be used in any other action other than the action in which these values are being grabbed, then these output values should be sent to the global sheet and not the local sheet.

Data Table

F3 Yes

	InvoiceAmount	AdjustmentAmount	Tonnage	Payables	ServerName	CreateShortPay
1	644.83	0		Yes	qa	No
2	1000	355.17		Yes	qa	No
3	1000	355.17		Yes	qa	Yes
4						

Global / AccountsPayable / GeneratePayables [GeneratePayables] / Step2Test [Step2Test] / S

Data Table | Missing Resources | Active Screen

Some applications need a lot of data to be entered into the application and in such cases we might run out of the fields in the Global Sheet. If this is the situation you can plan on using the local sheets of individual actions to drive the data into application. This is suitable only if you have an architecture where you are developing one action per screen and calling all the actions into a flow one after the other. In this situation you should make sure you add the code below on top of every action to sync between global row being executed and the corresponding local sheet row.

```
Datatable.GlobalSheet.GetCurrentRow
Datatable.LocalSheet.SetCurrentRow
```

Make sure that the reusable actions are set to run one iteration only if you are using the above code. To make the actions one iteration, right click on the action in the "Test Flow" from the Keyword view and select "Action Call Properties" and under the Run tab make sure it is the radio button "Run one iteration only" is selected.

If you don't take this care of synchronizing the local table's row with the Global row being executed, the script will always take the data from the first row of the local sheet which is not you want.

2.4. Data Sheet

It is one of the sheets in the Data Table. Example:.,Global and GeneratePayables, Step2Test (local action sheets) etc.

2.5. Object Repository

Object Repository (OR) is a collection of objects pertaining to the application under test. Example: All the text boxes, list boxes, images etc are stored in a file in QTP. This file is called the object repository. Each object will have the set of properties to identify that object uniquely in the application. At the time of execution, QTP identifies the objects on the screen by comparing them with the objects and their properties in the repository.

2.6. Function Library

Function is a QTP script wrapped into a VBScript. When we have a set of lines in QTP script, which have to be executed multiple times in the same script or in different scripts, we wrap them into a function and give them a name which would be a function name.

Function library is a set of such functions created for the entire project. For a project we may need functions like Login, Logoff and, CloseAllBrowsers etc. These functions should be written in a text file and then saved as a VB Script file (.vbs extension). This way we can have all the functions written at one place.

2.7. Initialization Script

Initialization script is an action which grabs the required variables and defines any environment variables required throughout the flow. This script should also launch the required applications. This should be the first action in the flow of actions. Initialization should also act as a cleanup script which means, when running the tests in the batch mode overnight, if the test fails for some reason in one of the test case (Global row execution), the test goes through all the steps in all the actions until the end of the flow of actions and when it comes to the next global row which is the fresh start of the new test case it should not stop or fail because of the existing windows of the application on the screen. The initialization script should have the cleanup process which should close all the existing windows of the application and should login freshly into the application so the script flow can continue with the new test case.

To run the tests in the batch mode go to Test settings from File Menu. Click on the Run node and select "Proceed to next step" from the list box which says "When error occurs during run session". This will ensure that all the steps in all actions are executed and the test does not stop.

See the picture below:

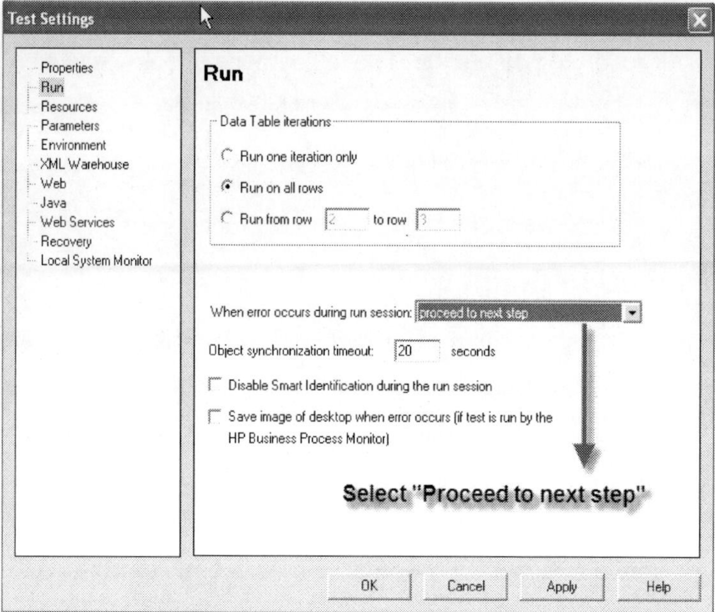

2.8. Environment Variables

Environment variables are the variables which can be defined and made available to the entire flow of actions or for just one action. Throughout the test run, the value of an environment variable remains the same, regardless of the number of iterations, unless you change the value of the variable programmatically in your script.

There are two types of environment variables:

a) Built-in: These are predefined by QTP. E.G. ActionIteration, OSVersion etc.
   The values of the Built-in environment variables can't be changed.
b) User-Defined: These are defined by the user as and when required.

2.9. Identifiers/Flags

Flags are the special identifier fields in the data sheet based on which the logic can be built into the actions. For instance, if there are any state specific variations in the test cases which we want to verify within the test, we can have a flag "State" as a field in the data table and based on the value of that field, we can build the logic in the script. We can also use the environment variables as flags where possible.

QTP Scripting Guidelines

3.1. Test Settings

1. The flow setting should always be "Run on all rows" so that all the test cases can be run without interruption. This setting can be made by going to File → Settings →Run Node → in the data table iterations section, make sure that "Run on all rows" is selected.

Run Tab of Test Settings:

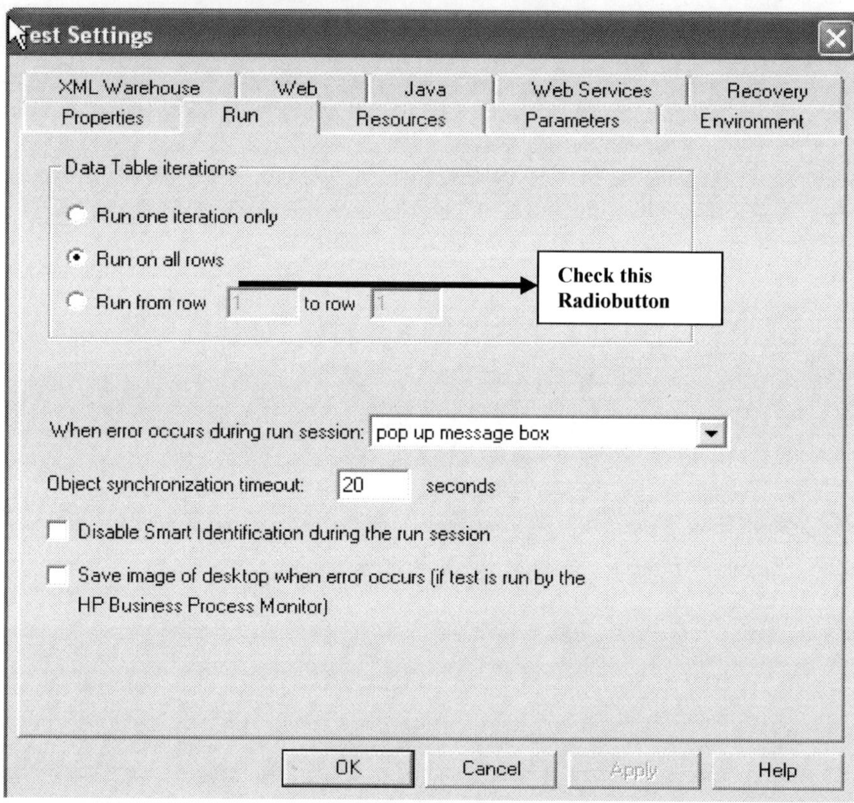

2. Resources to be used with the flow have to be set in the "Resources" node of the Test Settings.
3. Always store all the functions used in the project together in a VB Script file. This file should be then attached to QTP using the Function libraries section of the Resources. Go to File→ Test Settings →Resources tab

and in the “Libraries” section click on the green “+” sign. This will allow you to browse the VB Script file.

4. The data table for the flow should be set to “Other” and the data table/excel file which has the data, for all the test cases has to be attached by browsing the file. You may choose the default for data table if you are creating a new data table and in this case your Global sheet should have the values to be supplied into application. Typically each row of Global sheet will represent a test case.

3.2. Object Repository:

We can have any number of Shared Object Repositories associated with an action. In QTP 10 all the objects will be recorded into the local repository and we need to export the objects from local repository into the shared object repository by opening the object repository and selecting File Menu and selecting “Export Local Objects”. You need to specify the name for the shared object repository in which you want to save these objects.

3.3. Associating multiple Object Repositories for a test:

Open the object repository of the action and click on the icon Associate Repositories  on the tool bar. Associate repositories window opens. Click on the green “+” sign and browse the shared object repository and select it. All the actions which are available in that script will be shown in the Available Actions section of that window. Select the action which you to associate the repositories to and click on the “>” arrow to send it to the “Associated Actions” section of the window. This will ensure that the actions in the associated actions will have access to all the objects in the associated object repositories. You can associate any number of object repositories.

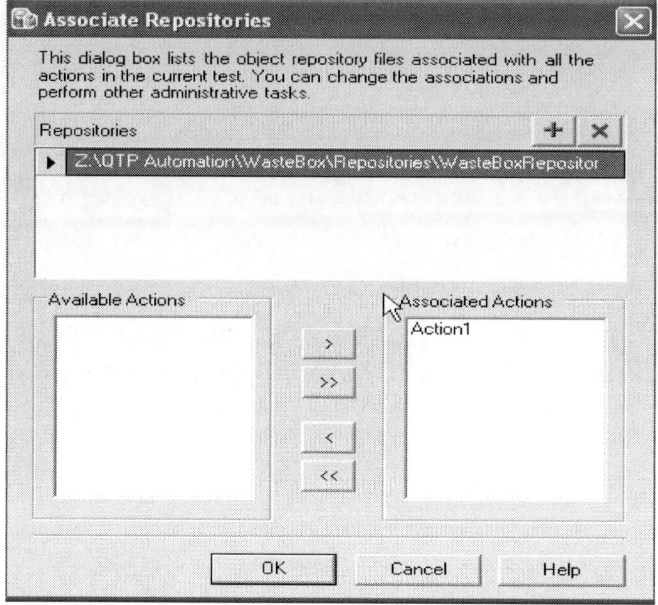

3.4. Adding New Objects to the shared Object Repository:

Whenever you add any new objects to the script either through recording or through the Object repository option the new objects will be added to the local repository for that script. In order to add these to the shared object repository which is used by all scripts we need to go to Resources menu and select Object Repository Manager and open the shared object repository for your project. When you open the shared repository it will be read-only. Click on Enable Editing icon on the toolbar to make it read-write.

3.5. Declaring Environment Variables

Environment variables can be declared from the
File→Settings→Environment Node

1. Under variable type drop down we have two options Built-in and User-defined. Built-in Environment variables can be used as it is from anywhere in the scripts by calling it.
   E.G. **OperatingSystem = Environment("OS")** will get the Operating system being used into the variable OperatingSystem.
2. We can declare a User-defined variable right from the initialization script.
   Example: **Environment("ApplicationVersion") = ""** will create an environment variable "ApplicationVersion" without assigning any value to it. You can now use this variable throughout the flow.
   Example: if you want to assign a value to the environment variable, then say, **Environment("ApplicationVersion")="Centura"**. The environment variable will now have a value of "Centura". If you want to use a condition around this, you can use it as
   'If Environment("ApplicationVersion") = "Centura" Then'...

3. If you have some values which should be declared as constants, you can define them in an external XML file and call them into the scripts. You can't modify the values of these constants within the scripts/actions. The advantage of having this kind of external variables file is that you can store all the values at one place. To create the XML file with the environment variables, use the notepad and declare the values as tags. This file is then attached to the main flow in the File → Test settings →Environment under User-defined section by browsing the file.
   Example code to create XML file:

```
<Environment>
        <Variable>
                <Name>PolicyPlan</Name>
                <Value>Auto</Value>
        </Variable>
        <Variable>
                <Name>LegacyApplication</Name>
                <Value>Centura</Value>
        </Variable>
```

```
<Variable>
    <Name>NewApplication</Name>
    <Value>.Net</Value>
</Variable>
</Environment>
```

The following code grabs the Environment variable "NewApplication" into the local variable "Application" and displays it.

```
Application = Environment("NewApplication")
MsgBox Application
```

Snapshot of Environment Node:

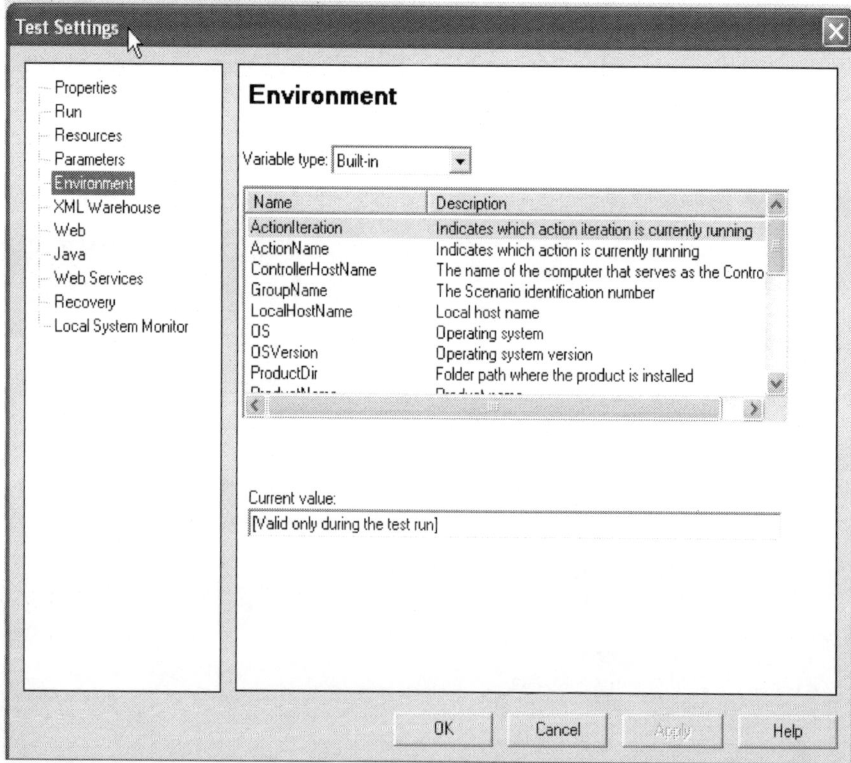

Note: The value of the Internal User defined environment Variable declared either from the environment node or declared programmatically can be changed, but the value of In-built or External environment variable coming from a text or xml file can't be changed.

3.6. Guidelines for Actions

3.6.1. Documentation

1. Include a header on the top of the Action explaining what the action does and specify any dependencies. This will help the automation developers in better understanding the purpose of each action in the flow and can utilize the same action when the need arises.

In the following example Test Purpose, Test Case Name, Pre-Requisites, Comments are explained.

```
'*****************************************************************************************************
'Test Purpose                    :          To test the functionality of creating and editing clients
'
'Test Case Name                  :          Create_Edit_Client
'
"Pre-requisites:                 :          Application should be launched before running this
                                            action.
"'Variables Used                 :          AutoID, Client Name
'
"Comments                        :          This action creates a client with the customer
                                            information and returns an client id.
'
"Change History                  :
'
"Date:          Changed/Created By:                    Reason:
"01/26/2007     Sridhar Reddy                          New Action
"
'Any changes done on this action should be documented in this Change History section.
'*****************************************************************************************************
```

2. Provide comments wherever required within in the script. This makes the code more meaningful and understandable. Comments can be added by starting a line with an apostrophe.

Example for comments:

```
'Click on Client Search link
Browser("OAKLEAF Acorn - Login").Page("OAKLEAF Acorn - Login").Frame("menu").Link("Search for Client").Click
CheckScreenID()
Browser("OAKLEAF Acorn - Login").Page("OAKLEAF Acorn - Login").Frame("mainBody").WebEdit("ClientID").Set Environment("ClientID")
Browser("OAKLEAF Acorn - Login").Page("OAKLEAF Acorn - Login").Frame("mainBody").WebButton("Search").Click

'Click on Client Main since the Client search's landing page is Locations tab.
Browser("OAKLEAF Acorn - Login").Page("OAKLEAF Acorn - Login").Frame("mainBody").Link("Client Main").

'Checking that the client title is displayed
CheckClientTitle()

'Creating client by using Create New Client button

Browser("OAKLEAF Acorn - Login").Page("OAKLEAF Acorn - Login").Frame("mainBody").WebButton("Create New Client").Click
CreateClient()

'Editing Client Information
'Click on Client Search link and search the client we just created
Browser("OAKLEAF Acorn - Login").Page("OAKLEAF Acorn - Login").Frame("menu").Link("Search for Client").Click
Browser("OAKLEAF Acorn - Login").Page("OAKLEAF Acorn - Login").Frame("mainBody").WebEdit("ClientID").Set Environment("ClientID")
Browser("OAKLEAF Acorn - Login").Page("OAKLEAF Acorn - Login").Frame("mainBody").WebButton("Search").Click
```

Comment Line in green

3.6.2. Building Actions

1. For the automation purposes, it is recommended that the application be classified into various parts and the actions be scripted around the individual screens. For instance, each screen will have one script built to address that screen, and only one reusable action in that script which in turn is called into a main script thereby making a flow of the entire application. This way of breaking your automation scripts into pieces based on the screens in the application will help the automation engineer to fix the scripts very easily if there is a change in any particular screen without disturbing the other scripts.

   Note: This method may not suite every application.

2. Each project should have an initialization script/action which should grab the environment variables, application path to open, User Defined variables from TestDirector or Quality Center and the application cleanup process like closing all the open browsers or windows.

3. Actions should always be created in QTP and then saved in QualityCenter. Do not use QualityCenter for creating and launching actions as it can be very time consuming.

4. When creating actions always record objects in the sequence on the application page and logic of the test case. If more than one QTP developer is working on the same project, make sure you learn all the objects in the application into the shared repository which is used by all the developers. This will ensure that all the objects are already available and developers can work with their scripts even when the object repository is locked by another user. Another work around is to have one Shared Object Repository for each developer and merge the repositories every week.

5. Most of the time, you may find that QTP generates its own names for the objects. Always rename the objects in the Object Repository. The name chosen should identify the object represented on the application. Use screen name separated by underscore and object name. This is a one time job and you do not have to change the name next time you record on the same object.

6. When deleting any statement from the script, delete the corresponding object(s) first from the repository if they are no longer required by any of the automation developers. This way we can manage the size of the Object Repository.

7. If something is specific to a line of business then make sure to encapsulate it in an "If ..Then..Else" statement.

8. Always declare all the variables that you use in your script at the top.

9. Use "Option Explicit" on the top. This will keep a check on variables being used without declaring them first.

10. Always add the data columns in the data sheet as per the sequence of the objects in the action.

11. Indentation of the code is required for readability purpose.

Example Code:

The correct way:

```
If X=Y Then

        Y= Z
Else
        Y = A
End If
```

Wrong way:

```
If X=Y Then

Y= Z
Else Y = A
End If
```

12. Text comparisons should use UCase() or LCase() for the values that are compared. This will address any problems due to case sensitivity.

3.6.3. Using Test Parameters and Action Parameters

Test Parameters and Action parameters is another way of providing the input values to the test and actions and also used to store output value.

To create a Test Parameter:

3.6.3.1. Input Parameters:

Open a New Test. Go to File-->Settings, and go to 'Parameters' node. Then click on '+' sign. Enter a meaning name to the parameter (for instance to give the Application Under Test (AUT) path as part of the test input parameter) 'AUT_Path' and its Default Value as “http://www.onsitetraining.net” (Application URL). Set the type of this parameter to string.

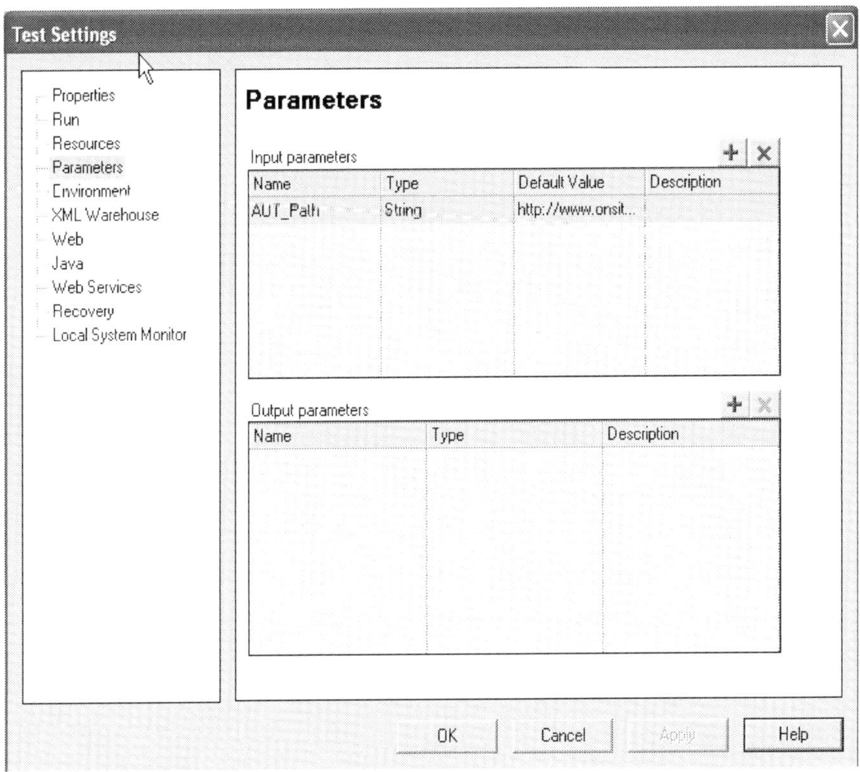

This creates a Test Parameter. Now from the Keyword View right click on “Action1” and select 'Action Properties'. “Action Properties” window opens. Click on “Parameters” tab. Click on '+' sign. Enter a name of the Action parameter as for instance, “ApplicationURL” and set its Type as string and leave the default value as blank.

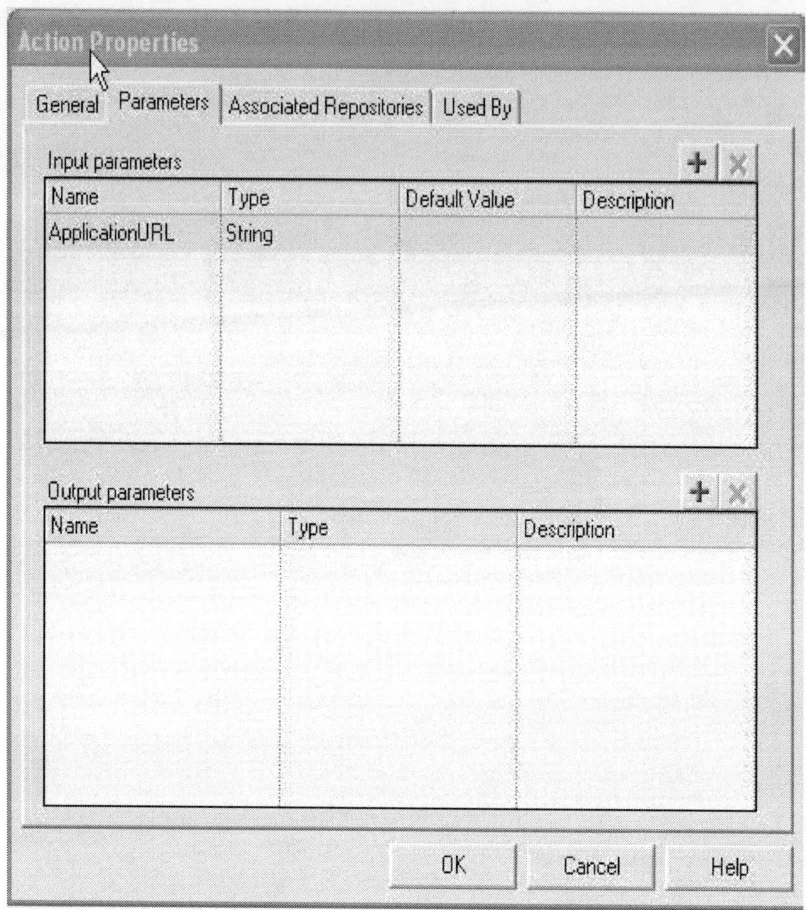

Click “OK” to come out of that window. In the Keyword View go to the Test Flow level by selecting “Test Flow” from the actions dropdown list and then select “Action1” from the flow, right click on “Action1” and select “Action Call Properties”. 'Action Call Properties' window opens. Now go to 'Parameter Values' Tab. You will see the 'ApplicationURL' action parameter which we created earlier. Click in the “Value” heading, it will show a pound sign <#>. Click on that <#> sign to open 'Value Configuration Options' window.

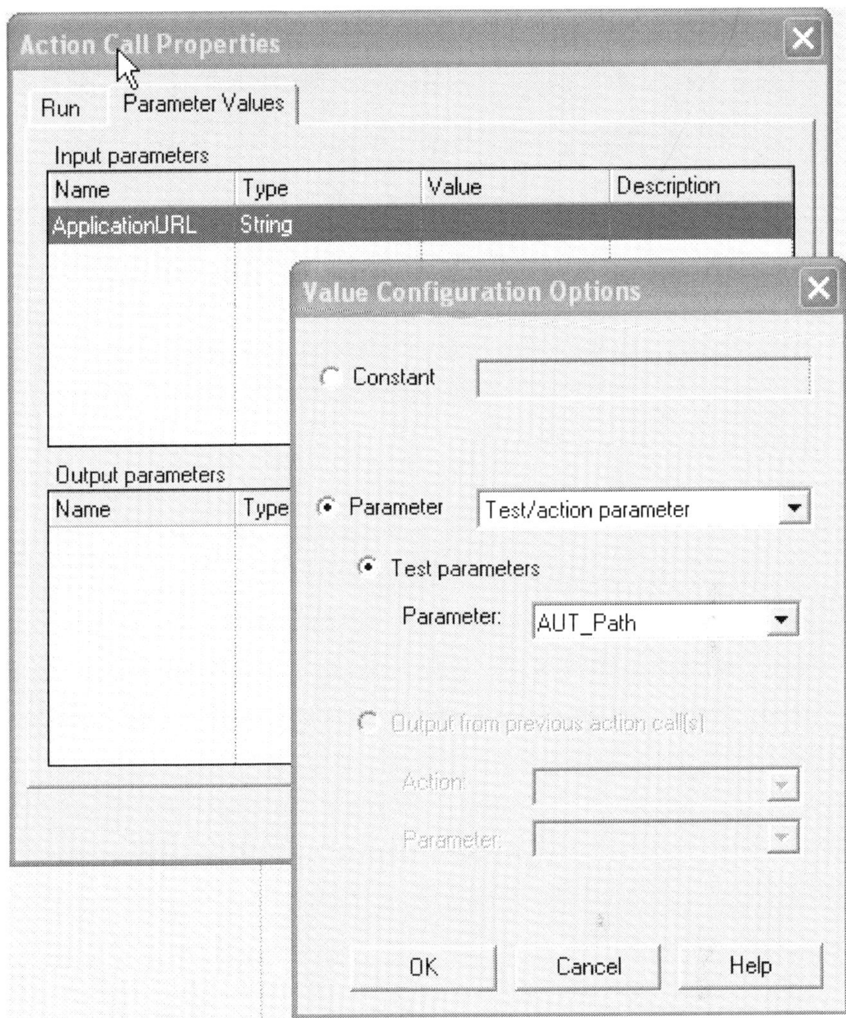

Select "Parameter" radio button and select "Test/action Parameter" from the dropdown list. All the test parameters we create will be displayed in this list. Select "AUT_Path" from Parameter dropdown. This is the test parameter we created at the test level for specifying the URL of the application under test. Once you click on "OK" to come out of 'Value Configuration Options' window, in the 'Action Call Properties' window, under 'Value' it will show <AUT_Path>. Click OK to accept that.

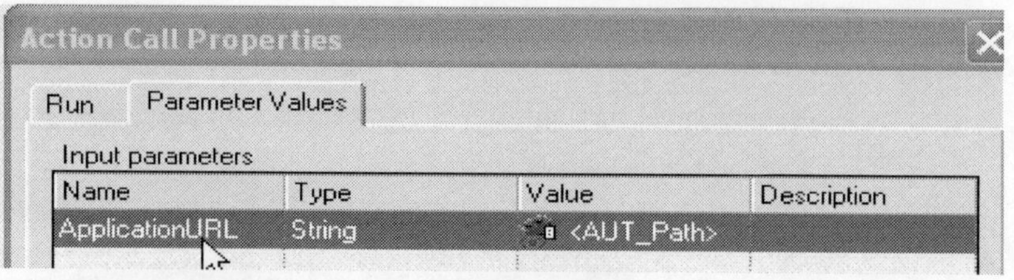

Now go to Expert View and test it by typing

MsgBox Parameter("ApplicationURL") and run the test. It will display "http://www.onsitetraining.net" in the message box which is the value we entered in the test parameter. Thus the action parameter is using the test parameter value as input.

Note: The action parameters should be declared in advance, if we want them to use the test parameter values. For the internal actions we can create the action parameters at anytime, but for the external actions called into the flow we can't create the action parameters in the flow and those parameters have to be defined in the original action, and once the parameter is defined they can utilize the test parameter values as input.

Action Parameters can take the values from the global sheet and the values stored in the action parameters of the parent action or parent test into which the action is called. They can also take the output value of the previous called action as the value of input parameter.

3.6.3.2. Output Parameters:

Output Parameters can be used to store the output values grabbed from the application. Example:

Parameter("Myoutput") = "This is the output parameter"

Msgbox Parameter("Myoutput")

Create the output parameters at the action level. Output parameters do not have a default value. We are assigning a text to that output parameter and displaying that value using message box command.

Let's illustrate this with another example. Create an output parameter called "MyLoginOutput" in the Login action and write the following code in the login action:

```
If Window("Flight Reservation").Exist(15) Then
        Parameter("MyLoginOutput") = "Pass"
            else
        Parameter("MyLoginOutput") = "Fail"
End If
```

Then open the "Order_Entry" action which follows the login action. In this action define an Input Action Parameter "MyLoginInput" without any default value.

Call these two actions into a script (Flow) one after the other.

Go to keyword view of the flow and right click on the "Order_Entry' action call and select "Action Call Properties" and then go to "Parameter Values" tab. You can see the input action parameter "MyLoginInput", defined in the "Order_Entry" action. Click on the value field and you will see the "#" sign appearing in the value field. Click on the "#' sign which will take you to the "Value Configutation Options" window. Now select the radio button "Parameter". Now you can see two radio buttons enabled.

a) Parent action parameters
b) Output from previous action call(s)

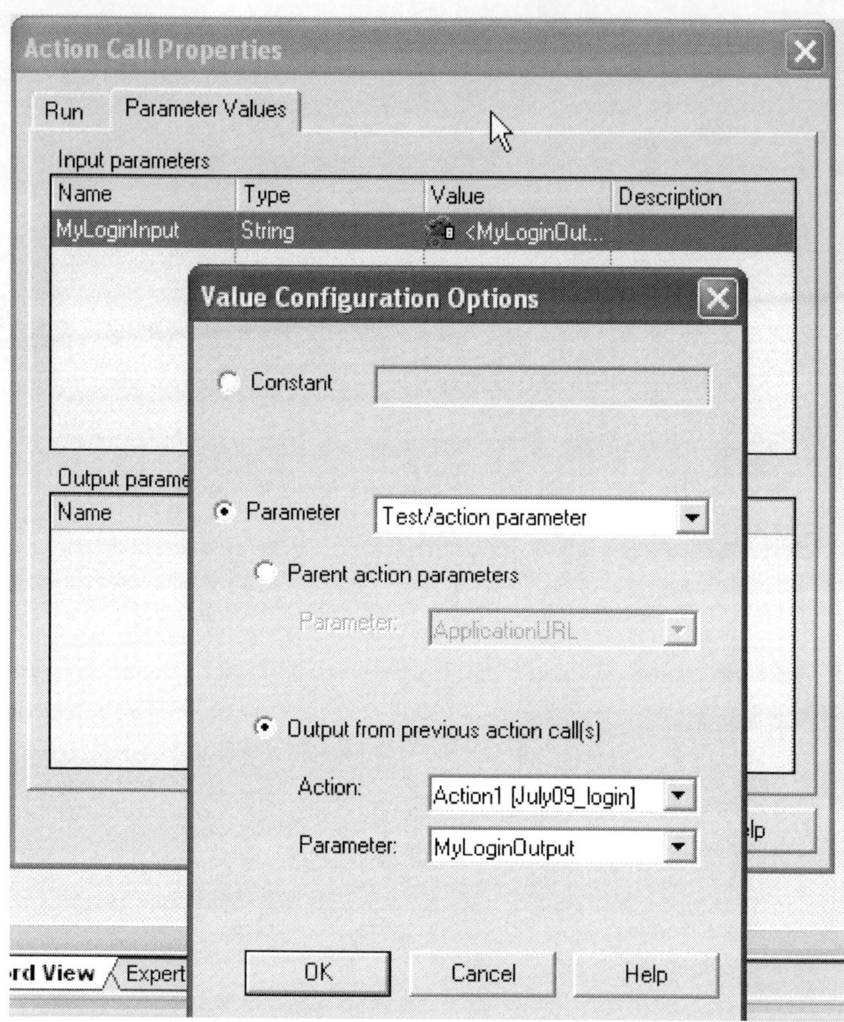

Select the second radio button “Output from previous action call(s). You can now see the action name in the “Action” drop down and the Login action’s output parameter in the “Parameter” drop down. Select the Login action from the Action drop down and the “MyLoginOutput” from the parameter drop down and click “OK”. The input parameter for the Order_Entry action will now take the output parameter value from the Login action.

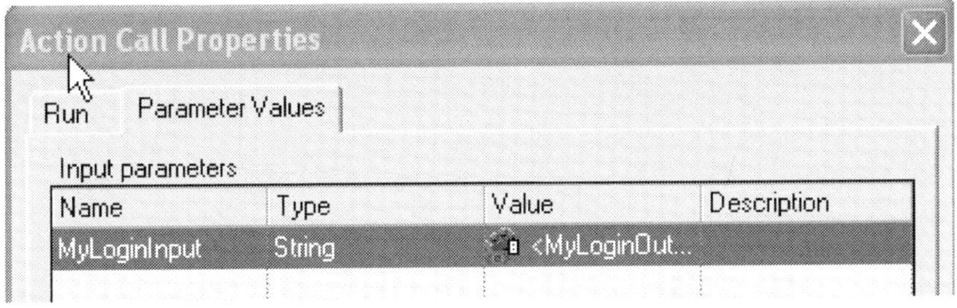

Close the Action Call Properties window by clicking "OK".

Now you can use the output value of the Login action and route your Order_Entry action depending on the output value of the login action parameter.

3.7. Guidelines for Flows

3.7.1. Creation of Flow

1. When inserting a reusable action into the flow, always use the option "Call to Existing Action" and not the "Call to Copy of Action". This way, the called action will be **read only.** Any changes we need to make in the called actions should be made by opening that action. These changes are automatically applied in the flow as well.

2. When inserting a reusable action into the flow, make sure that all the actions are inserted at the same hierarchy. When inserting the reusable action from the keyword view place your cursor on the Action1 which is the flow action then select the radio button "After the Current Step". Make sure your cursor is placed on the Action1 every time you insert an action. Later you can move the reusable actions into the order you want them to be executed. When inserting the actions from the expert view place the cursor on line one which is empty and right click. Select "Action' and then "Insert call to existing" and browse the action to be inserting. Then for inserting the next action pull the action1 from the dropdown which will now show the

action which you inserted. Place the cursor on the line one and insert action from there.

3. "Call to Copy of Action" may be used in some situations where you want to use the code of the reusable action but need to make some changes to the code in order to accomplish a task. The updates made to the original action will not be updated in the flow when you use "Call to Copy of Action" option.

4. Most of the times there are test cases which are almost similar in flow of data except that the data changes according to the change in the test scenario like for example you might want to test the functionality of a piece of application for the state of Connecticut and in another test case you are testing the same functionality for the state of New York. There might be only slight variations in both the test cases. Such test cases have to be grouped together and the data for these test cases should be put in the Global Sheet of the data table in separate rows. This way each row of global sheet represents one test case.

5. Local table in most cases is used if the data is confined to a particular reusable action only or if a particular portion of the reusable action has to be repeated with multiple data, say for example, within a client account you are creating locations for that client and that client has 10 locations. In this case the location data has to be placed in the local sheet for that reusable action.

6. Local table of each reusable action should be editable from the flow. The data entered from the flow into this local sheet is not updated in the original action. This way the reusable action can be best used if you want to call the same reusable action into a different flow. The data is tied to the flow not to the action. To do this, after inserting the

action, right click on the action in the Keyword view to go to action properties of the external/reusable action and in the External Action tab's Data Table Parameters section, select the radio button "Use a local, editable copy".

Snapshot of Action Properties:

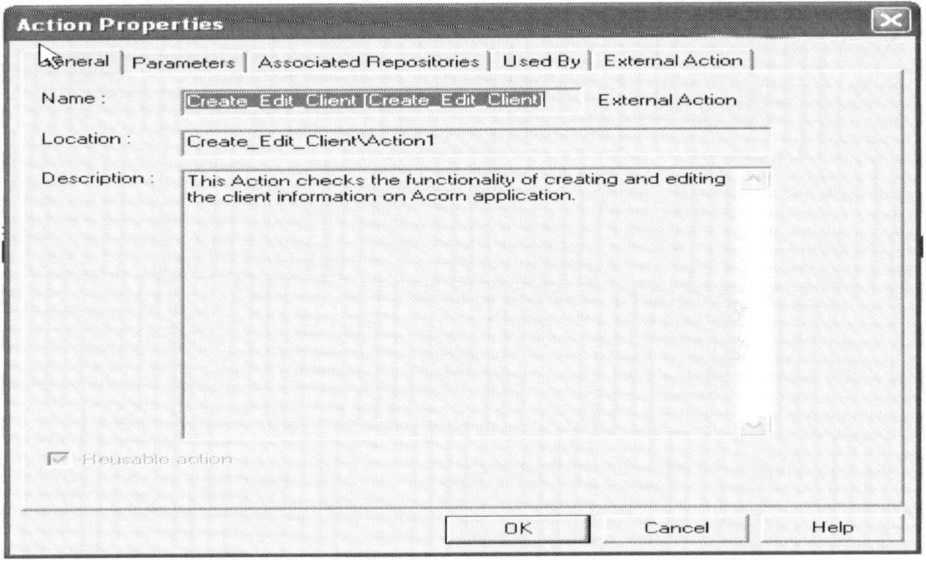

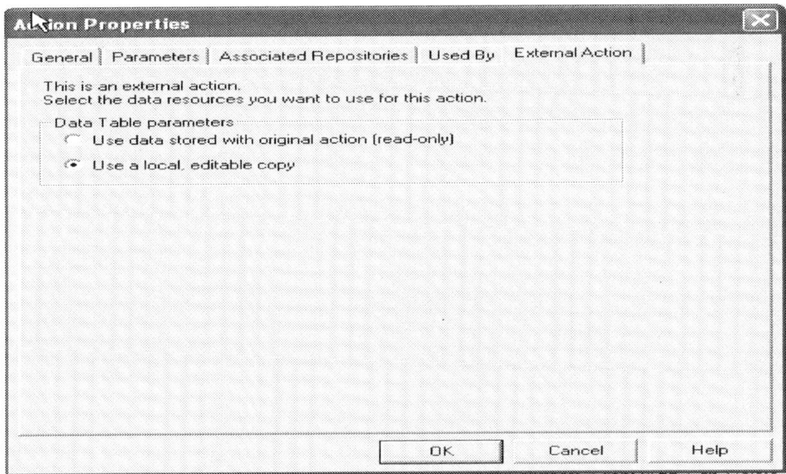

7. If an expected screen doesn't show up in any of the actions within the flow, then you might have to logoff and close all the windows and

launch the next global row. In such case this logic has to be built into a function Example: ScreenCheck(ScreenName). In this example ScreenCheck is the function name which takes a parameter called "ScreenName" which is the expected screen name. If for any reason the screen does not appear, this function has the code to skip the execution of that global row and go to the next global row or test case. Such function call has to be placed in every reusable action at the start of the action. This will ensure that the test flow execution is not stopped totally if there is a failure in one test case.

The flow will be something like the one shown below.

Snapshot of the Flow

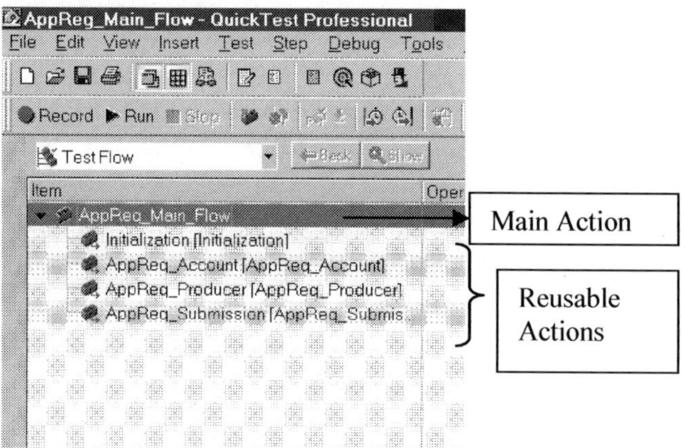

In the snapshot shown above, the name of the script is AppReg_Main_Flow which acts as the flow of actions, there is a main action AppReg_Main_Flow which is not reusable. It calls four reusable actions, Initialization, AppReg_Account, AppReg_Producer and AppReg_Submission sequentially.

3.7.2. Naming Convention for Flow

The name of the flow should be separated by underscore for easy understanding. It should have the application name embedded in the name.

3.7.3. Maintenance of Flow

1. Maintenance of the flow is required when a new screen is added to the application. A new reusable action has to be created for every new screen and called into the flow at the correct place.

2. If a screen is deleted from the application and we no longer need that screen we should remove the corresponding reusable action from the flow.

3.8. Guidelines for Object Repository Management

3.8.1. Object Repository:

1. Object Repository is the place where all the objects of the application being automated reside. As we record the key strokes on the application the objects are added to the local repository of the script.

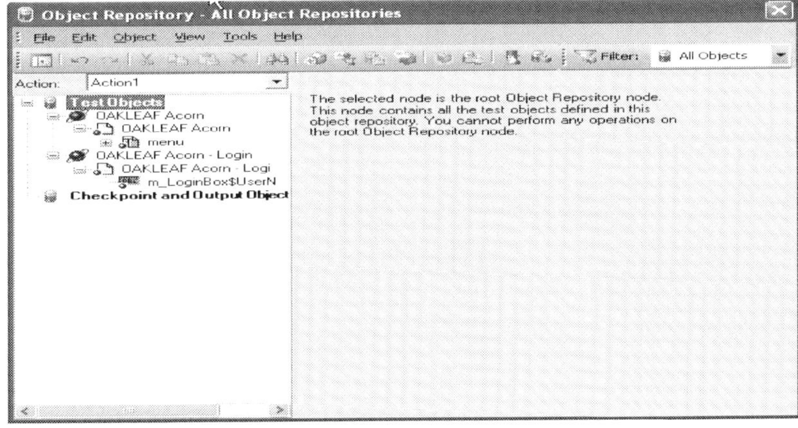

2. There should be one Object Repository per application/project. This makes it easy for automation engineer to change the object descriptions or add/delete objects when changes are made to the application. The objects which are in one script's local repository can't be accessed by the other script. We need to make a common repository in order for them to be shared across the scripts. To do this, open the object repository from the "Resources" menu and select "Object Repository". You will be seeing all the objects you recorded on, in the object repository.

3.8.2. Creating a Shared Object Repository:

From the File menu of the object repository window select Export Local Objects. You will be asked to enter a name for the shared object repository you are going to create. Give the name and click save. The shared object repot repository will be created.

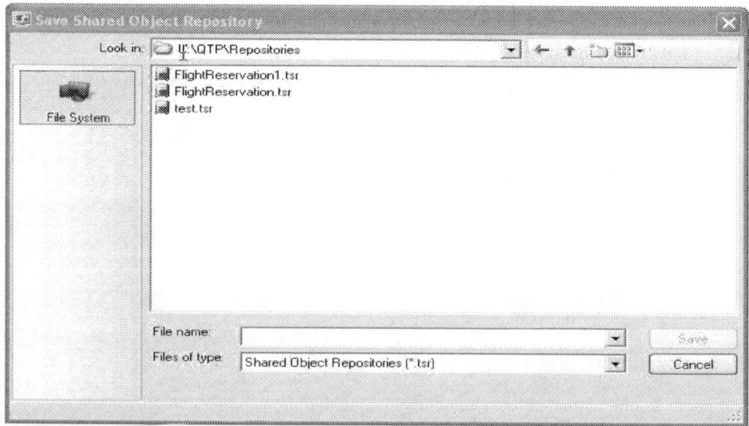

Then from the "Resources" menu select "Associate Repositories" where you can select the shared object repository by clicking on the "+" sign and selecting the shared object repository.

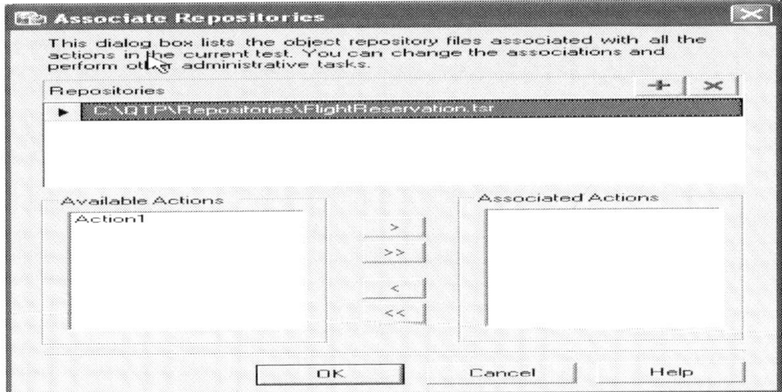

Then select the Action name in the Available Actions section and click the right arrow button to send the action to the Associated Actions section and then the repository is associated to that action. Always use the relative path and not the absolute path for object repository reference. This will be explained and illustrated later in this book.

3. All the actions and flow should be using the same shared OR. This will ensure that the objects recorded for the entire application will be at one place.

4. Always keep a daily backup copy of the Object Repository on your local hard drive. There might be instances where the OR gets corrupted.

3.8.3. Renaming Objects in Object Repository:

From the “Resources” menu select “Object Repository Manager”. Open the shared object repository by using File →open and browsing the repository. This will be Read-only and can’t be edited. Click on the “Enable Editing” icon on the toolbar which makes the shared object repository editable.

Find the object which you want to rename by using the pointing hand icon on the toolbar and point to the object in your application. This will bring the focus to that object in the shared object repository.
Right click the object name and choose rename
Enter the new name and hit enter or click anywhere in the area.
Click ok
Save your changes.

Prior to deleting code that refers to an object in Object Repository, delete the object from the repository if that object is no longer required in the project. This helps in keeping the size of the object repository to the minimum size.

3.8.4. Using Repository Parameters:

Sometimes objects can't be identified using the physical properties alone and even after applying the regular expression to the object properties. In such cases we can use the Repository Parameter to drive the physical property of such objects.

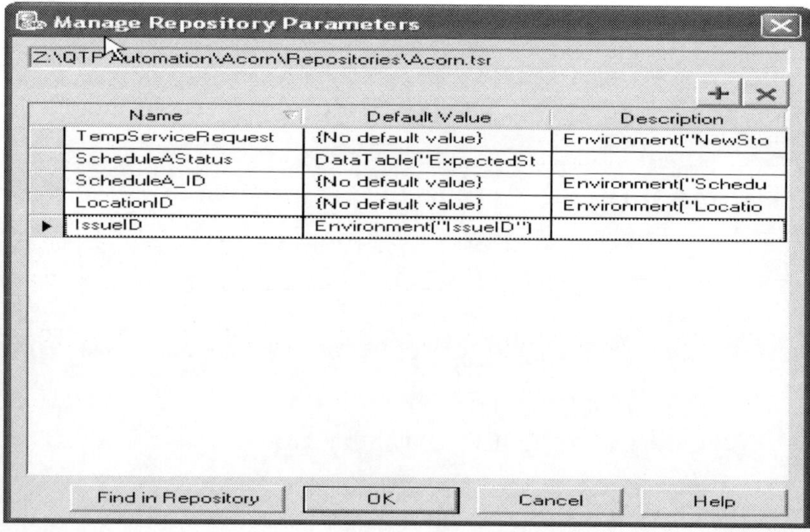

3.8.5. Defining Repository Parameters:

Open the shared object repository from the "Object Repository Manager" and from tools menu of that window select "Manage Repository Parameters".

Manage Repository Parameters window opens. Click on the "+" sign and you will see "Add Repository Parameter" window.

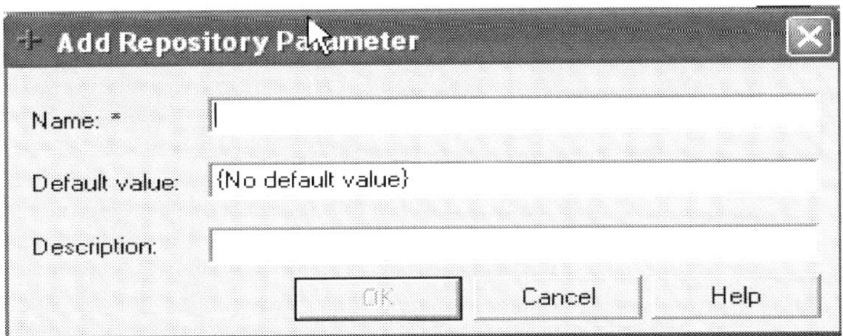

In the "Name" field give the name of the parameter. You can give any meaningful name. In the "Default value" field give the statement to populate the value. The two most common sources can be a data table or an Environment Variable. Refer to the picture below for how to declare the default value of the parameter.

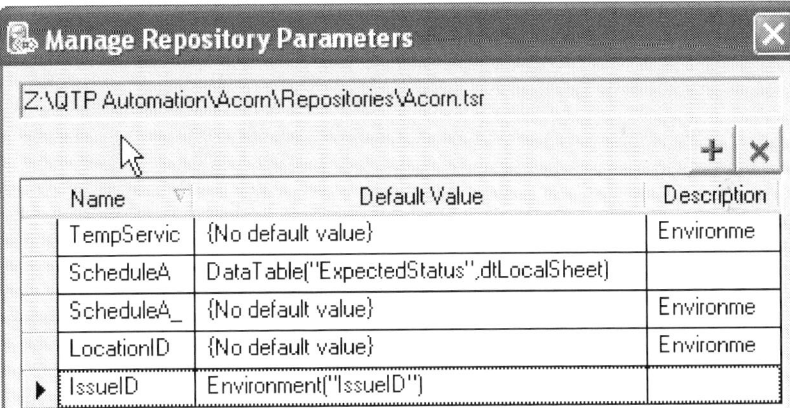

Name	Default Value	Description
TempServic	{No default value}	Environme
ScheduleA	DataTable("ExpectedStatus",dtLocalSheet)	
ScheduleA_	{No default value}	Environme
LocationID	{No default value}	Environme
IssueID	Environment("IssueID")	

From the repository manager, select the object for which you want to use the repository parameter and click on the physical property value field.

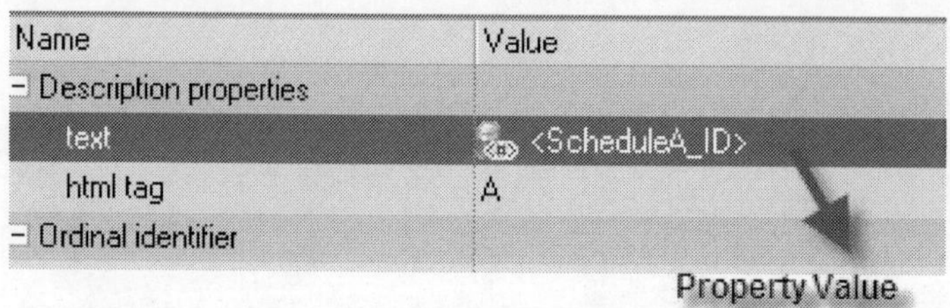

Repository Parameter window opens. Select the radio button "Parameter" and you will see all the repository parameters you defined previously from "Manage Repository Parameters" window.

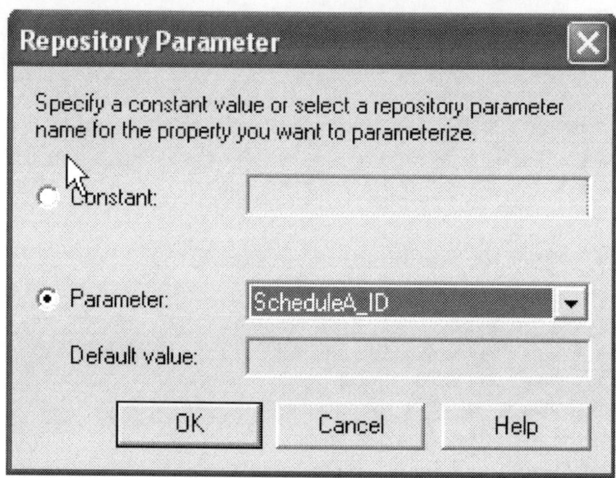

Select the appropriate parameter and click "OK" button. When this object needs to be identified, QTP uses the repository parameter to identify that object on the application.

3.9. Object Identification:

Object identification is a method of instructing QTP to recognize the various objects in the application. Usually QTP can identify the objects uniquely for most of the applications/objects, but for some applications this may not be true. In this scenario we need to tweak the Object Identification settings of QTP to learn extra properties or custom properties defined in the application, for recognizing the objects uniquely.

In order to do this, Go to Tools →Object identification and select the environment (windows, web etc). This will give you all the possible type of objects in that environment like Edit boxes, check boxes etc. Select the type of object you have problem recognizing uniquely. QTP will show you the mandatory and assistive properties which are grabbed and used currently for that object. You can select the extra properties which are already defined in the application for that kind of object by clicking on the green "+" sign and selecting the required properties. If you still have the problem of recognition then you need to find out the unique property defined for that object type from the development team and Add that custom property by clicking "New" in the Add/Remove properties window of Object identification. For example if the custom property name is "RefGen", you can click "New" and give the new property name as "attribute/RefGen". When you record next time on that kind of object the new properties will be automatically grabbed. If you want to update the existing objects run the test in the Update Run mode and select the checkbox Update Object Properties.

Note: The changes you make in the Object Identification will affect everyone working on that machine. These changes should be applied universally on all the machines you intend to run the regression tests. These are QTP setting changes not the script changes.

QTP is usually good at object recognition, but when you see that an object is not being recognized by QTP the object identification has to be tweaked. QTP has a mechanism of Smart identification which has to be tweaked and the properties with which you want to identify an object has to be specified in Smart Identification so that when there are slight variations in the object properties, QTP can invoke the Smart ID and recognize that object. Though invoking the Smart ID will make the test execution slow, it is very essential to run the test smooth and without failure. Smart Identification configuration can be made by going to Tools →Object Identification and checking the Smart Identification check box. Then hit the Configure button. This has to be repeated for every environment we use, like Standard Windows, .Net Web Forms, .Net Window Forms and Web.

The following snapshot shows different environments available for us based on the Add-ins loaded.

Snapshot of Object Identification Tab

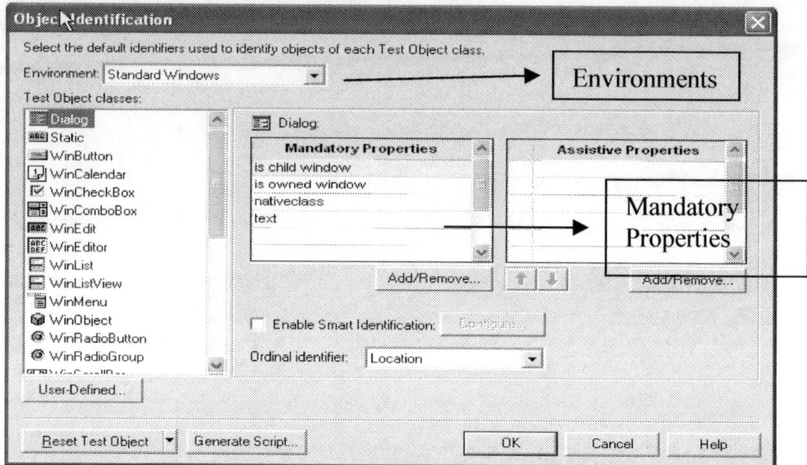

3.10. Guidelines for Data Table Management

3.10.1. Creation of Data Table

1. Store all the input data in the Global Table which is attached to the "Main Flow". The output data from the application which is used by any other action should be stored in the Global Sheet and any output data that is used in the same action can be stored in the local sheets of the corresponding action. Parameterize all the data and avoid hard coding of the values within the script. Each row of the Global sheet should represent a test case/test scenario.

2. Date table option for the actions should be set to "Default" initially so that when you save the action, a table with the name "default.xls" is created for every action you create. After preparing the Global Data

Table, change this option to "Other" and select the Global Data Table which is uploaded to QualityCenter.

3. Keep a copy of Data Table for every action that you are using on your local drive for quick reference. You can Right Click on the Data Table and choose File -->Export. Save it to your local drive.

4. When you create a flow, do not hook the Data Tablc prior to calling all the actions. Create the flow first, so that you have correct bindings of local data sheets with respective actions. Action local table will have the same name as the action name. Then Export the Data Table to the local drive and save it with a name based on the flow's name. This exported data table will now have **one Global sheet** and all the action **local sheets as tabs**. Any data which was present in the action's global sheet will be now appearing in the Global sheet of the data table. Close the flow after saving the changes. Open the Data Table in Excel and move any global Flags you find in the action's global data sheet in the front. Prefer to maintain the same order of the flags in the Flow as you encounter them in the actions.

5. Once the Data Table is prepared, upload it to QualityCenter in the designated folder. Open the flow again. Attach the newly created Data Table to the flow. To attach the excel sheet to the script, go to "Settings" from File menu and navigate to "Resources" tab and select the radio button "Other" in the data table section. Then browse the excel sheet you uploaded to Quality Center.

3.10.2. Data Table Naming Conventions

6. Use detailed Camel naming convention when naming the fields related to the object on the application you are referring to. Use

underscore as separator between the various parts for example, “Quick_Test_Professional”. Avoid cutting the names as it helps to associate the name with the field on the Application later.

Quality Center Guidelines

Quality Center Guidelines:

1. Always fill up details tab of the action in Quality Center when you use the action in a flow. This will help in maintaining the flows.
2. When an action is in the development phase keep the status as in design. As soon as the action is ready, change the status to Ready. If for some reason the action needs to be fixed change the status to "Repair". This will ensure to know which actions are under development and which ones are completed.

3. Any variables to be created in Quality Center for better managing the test execution should be well planned before building the flow. These variables can be grabbed into the Initiation script and can be used for executing the flow.

4. After flow has been created, include the details and dependencies of the flow in the details tab in Quality Center.

4.1. Managing Tests from Quality Center

1. To secure the usage of the tool, users should be created in Quality Center with QA Tester privileges for all the automation engineers. All the users have to be added to the projects on which they are working.

2. The site administration and project administration users and passwords should be setup. There should be a main Site Administrator and a backup Site Administrator. Easy reach of Site administrator is very important, as some times the user login does not get disconnected normally and the test gets locked, and we need to kill the process from site admin.

3. Automation engineers should have the Project Administration (not Site Administrator) privileges to create any User Defined variables in QualityCenter.

4. “Test Plan” part of the Quality Center should be well used by creating the required folders and saving the corresponding elements in them. For example: The actions folder should have all the reusable actions for that project/application and Flows folder should have the Flows saved in them. This ensures easy accessibility.

The following snapshot shows an example of organizing the folders in Quality Center for an application:

Snapshot of Folder structure in Quality Center

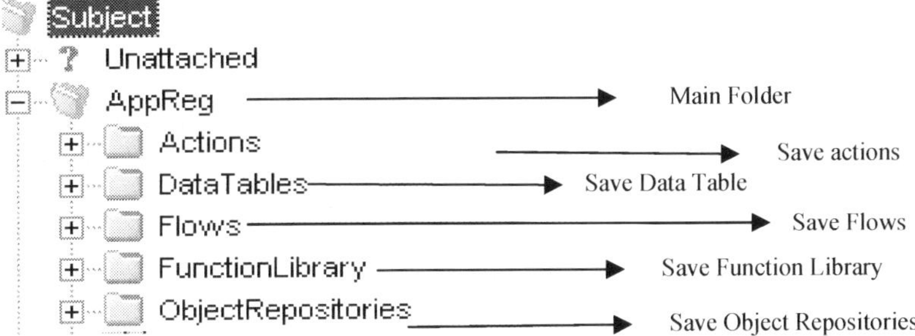

5. In order to better manage the test execution from Quality Center, create some User Defined fields in the Test Set and grab those variables into QTP. For example: Start Row, End Row, TestEnvironment etc.

4.2. *Managing Test Sets*

6. In order to keep track of the results from each release, name the test sets with the release date in it. Provide the dependencies if any in the Details portion of the Test Set properties.

7. The tests will always be run through Quality Center. This will enable us to compare the result history for every release.

8. Since QTP results take a heavy volume of disk space on the Quality Center server flush the results from the test set from time to time, keeping only the results from past one year releases.

References

HP QuickTest Professional User Manual

Index

Made in the USA